Country Style
Sewing

FOR THE HOME

Country Style Sewing

FOR THE HOME

CHILTON BOOK COMPANY
RADNOR · PENNSYLVANIA

Contents

Cushion cover~ups

Cushion pads need not always be encased in their traditional zipped covers, but can be wrapped in a number of ways, using various decorative fastening techniques. Generous bows, fabric-covered buttons, Velcro studs topped with silk flowers, and laced ribbon ties are all practical, but stylish ways of securing a cushion cover. Rather than concealing these fastenings as you would

a zip, make them a main feature of the cushion cover design.

Most furnishing cottons are suitable for making the cushion covers, but choose a fabric to complement the cushion design; for example, a soft floral print is ideal for the silk flower cushion, while a striped or checked fabric works well with the geometric lines of the envelope design.

▲ Creative covers
Leave ordinary zipped covers in the shade by making full use of decorative fastenings and your favourite fabrics to create a range of eye-catching cushions. Any one of these imaginative designs will give an instant lift to a plain chair, sofa or even a bedspread.

DOUBLE BOW CUSHION

Materials

Fabric measuring 104 × 43cm (41 × 17in); a print with a small and simple repeated motif works well with this design

Grossgrain ribbon in a contrast colour, 4m (4½yds) long and 4cm (1½in) wide

Sewing threads

Cushion 40 × 40cm (15¾ × 15¾in)

1 Cutting and hemming Cut the rectangle of fabric into two pieces, each one measuring 52 × 43cm (20½ × 17in). Along one of the short edges of one piece of fabric, turn in a 1.5cm (⅝in) hem to the wrong side and stitch in place; repeat on the other piece of fabric.

2 Joining the pieces Place the cushion pieces together, right sides facing and with the hemmed edges matched up. Stitch down the remaining short edge to join the front and back pieces together, allowing a 1.5cm (⅝in) allowance.

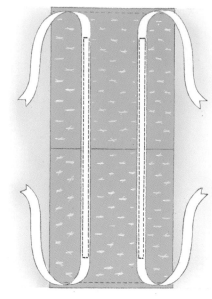

3 Attaching the ribbons Open out the cushion pieces to lie flat with right sides face up. Cut the ribbon into two equal lengths of 2m (2¼yds), and shape the ends by cutting out a small 'V'. Pin one length down each long side of the cushion, 10cm (4in) in from the edge and parallel to it; stitch down both sides of the ribbon, stopping with a line of stitching across it, 12cm (4¾in) from the top and bottom edges of the cushion.

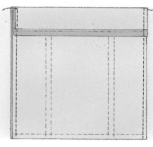

4 Finishing the cushion Refold the cushion with right sides together, tucking in the unstitched ends of the ribbons. Fold over 9cm (3½in) of the top edge of the cushion and stitch down both sides, 1.5cm (⅝in) in from the edges to join the sides and form a flap. Turn through to the right side and insert the cushion pad, tucking it under the flap. Tie the ribbons into two generous bows.

Double bow cushion

Lace-up cushion

ENVELOPE CUSHION

Materials

Patterned fabric 43 × 42cm (17 × 16½in)

Plain fabric in a contrasting colour, measuring 80 × 42cm (31½ × 16½in)

Binding in a contrasting colour, 2m (2¼yds) long

Ribbon to match the binding, 80cm (31½in) long and 2.5cm (1in) wide

Sewing threads

Cushion 40 × 40cm (15¾ × 15¾in)

1 Preparing the centre piece Lay out the patterned piece of fabric, wrong side up. Turn in a 1.5cm (⅝in) hem along the two short sides.

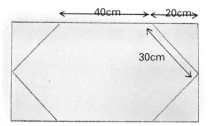

2 Cutting out the outer piece Cut off the corners from the plain fabric rectangle to form a hexagon of the dimensions shown: measure 20cm (8in) in from both short sides along the top and bottom edges, and mark with tailor's chalk; then measure halfway up the short side edges and mark the spot. Join these points to form the hexagon and carefully cut it out.

3 Sewing on the binding Lay out the plain fabric and centre the patterned piece of fabric over it, with wrong sides together. Pin and tack the two pieces together along the top and bottom edges. Beginning at one of the far tips of the hexagon, pin and then sew the binding around the raw edges, joining the patterned and plain fabric together along the top and bottom edges.

Envelope cushion

Silk flower cushion

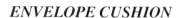

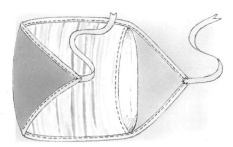

4 **Attaching the ribbon** Cut the ribbon into two lengths of 40cm (15¾in). Take one length and stitch it to the wrong side of one of the outer flaps; use tiny stitches which do not show on the right side. Repeat for the second ribbon length. Shape the ribbon ends by cutting out a small 'V'. Slip the cushion pad in behind the patterned panel, fold in the two flaps and tie the ribbons in a bow.

SILK FLOWER CUSHION

Materials

Fabric measuring 75 × 71cm (29¼ × 28in); an all-over floral print complements this design perfectly
Six fabric flowers in silk or imitation silk and in a toning shade; if you prefer, use bows or fabric-covered buttons instead of flowers
Six pairs Sew 'n' Sew Velcro coins
Sewing threads
Cushion pad 45 × 36cm (17¾ × 14¼in)

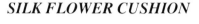

1 **Forming a tube** Fold the fabric in half, with shortest edges and right sides together. Pin and stitch these edges together to form a tube, taking a 1.5cm (⅝in) seam allowance.

2 **Hemming the ends** Turn in a 1.5cm (⅝in) hem to the wrong side, along the raw edges of the fabric at both ends of the tube; stitch in place.

3 **Folding in the cushion sides** Fold back 7cm (2¾in) of the fabric at each end of the tube towards its centre; do not stitch, but press the folds to hold the fabric in place. This will eliminate the need for a seam running down the sides of the finished cushion cover.

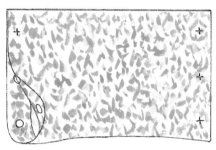

4 **Securing the cushion sides** Stitch three pairs of Velcro coin fastenings down each side of the cushion, over the folded hems, 4cm (1½in) in from the outer edges; the stitching will secure the folded sides. Turn the cushion through to the right side.

5 **Adding the flowers** Stitch one flower over each Velcro coin to hide the stitching. Slip the cushion into the tube and press the Velcro coins together to seal the cover.

LACE-UP CUSHION

Materials

Patterned fabric measuring 86 × 43cm (33¾ × 17in)
Plain fabric in a contrasting colour, measuring 55 × 10cm (21¾ × 4in)
Binding in a co-ordinating colour, 320cm (3⅝yds) long
Ribbon in a contrast shade to binding, 190cm (2yds) long and 2cm (¾in) wide
Basic eyelet kit available from most haberdashery departments
Sewing threads
Cushion 40 × 40cm (15¾ × 15¾in)

1 **Cutting out** Cut the rectangle of patterned fabric into two squares of 43cm (17in). Cut one square in half diagonally; the two triangles will form the front flaps of the cushion.

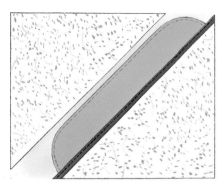

2 **Attaching contrast strip** Trim both ends of the contrast strip into a curve and turn under a 1.5cm (⅝in) hem along the curved edge. Pin and stitch the binding to the longest edge of one fabric triangle. Place the bound triangle edge over the raw straight edge of the contrast strip, so that they overlap by 2cm (¾in) and both lie face-up; tack together. Stitch the contrast strip to the triangle, but leave four gaps next to where the four eyelets will lie – ribbon will be laced through these gaps. Stitch binding to long edge of the other fabric triangle.

3 **Joining front to back** Position the triangles over the patterned fabric square, wrong sides together. Pin then stitch binding around cushion edges, joining front and back pieces. Slip-stitch diagonal slit together for 2cm (¾in) only, at both ends.

4 **Adding the ties** Use the eyelet kit to make four holes down each side of the diagonal slit in the front of the cushion, 8cm (3¼in) apart. Insert the cushion pad via the slit. Cut the ribbon into two equal lengths and shape the ends as usual. Thread the ribbon through the eyelets as shown and secure the cover with two bows.

BRODERIE ANGLAISE BOLSTER

Materials
Broderie anglaise fabric measuring 89 × 63cm (35 × 24¾in)
Fabric for the lining in a pastel shade, the same size as the broderie anglaise; use a reasonably stiff cotton fabric
Narrow broderie anglaise trimming 130cm (1½yds) long
Ribbon to match lining fabric, 150cm (1¾yds) long and 2.5cm (1in) wide
Sewing threads
Bolster 47cm (18½in) long and 18.5cm (7¼in) in diameter

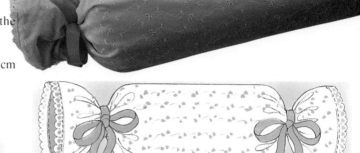

Broderie anglaise

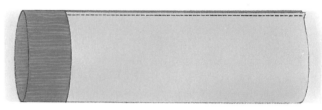

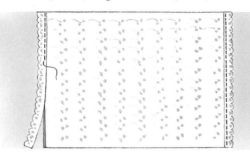

1 Joining the lining and trimming Place lining and broderie anglaise together, right sides facing and edges lined up. Pin and stitch along short edges, 1.5cm (⅝in) in from edge; turn through to right side. Cut broderie anglaise trimming into two equal lengths. Turning 1cm (⅜in) of the trimming's raw edge to the wrong side, if necessary, pin then stitch one length of trimming along one short end of the fabric, overlapping the two slightly and stitching through both the lining and the broderie anglaise; repeat on other short end.

2 Forming the bolster tube Fold the fabric in half lengthways, with the broderie anglaise sides together, and pin and stitch along the raw edge to form a tube, allowing a 1.5cm (⅝in) seam allowance.

3 Tying the ends Slip the bolster into the cover so that it lies in the centre. Cut the ribbon into two equal lengths of 75cm (29½in). Gather up the fabric at each end of the bolster and secure it with a ribbon bow.

MOIRE BOLSTER

Materials
Moiré fabric measuring 117 × 63cm (46 × 24¾in)
Velvet ribbon 150cm (1¾yds) long and 2.5cm (1in) wide
Narrow cord or **fabric tape** 170cm (1⅞yds) long and no wider than 1cm (⅜in)
Sewing threads
Bolster 47cm (18½in) long and 18.5cm (7¼in) in diameter

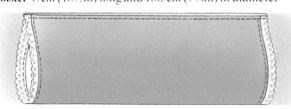

1 Forming the bolster tube Fold the fabric in half lengthways, with right sides together. Stitch the long edges together allowing a 1.5cm (⅝in) seam allowance. Fold in a 15cm (6in) hem at each end of the tube and press to hold it in place.

Moiré cushion

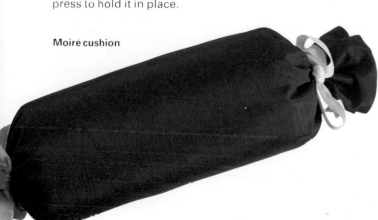

2 Making a casing for the pull cord Stitch round one end of the tube, 1.5cm (⅝in) out from the raw edge of the hem, leaving a small opening through which you can insert the pull cord. Measure 1.5cm (⅝in) out from the first line of stitching and stitch a second line around the end of the tube, to form a casing. Repeat at the other end of the tube. Cut the fabric tape or cord into two pieces of the same length and thread one through the casing at each end of the tube.

3 Finishing the bolster Turn the cover through to the right side and slide it over the bolster so that the bolster lies centrally. Slip your hand into one end of the bolster and draw up the pull cord or tape tightly, securing the ends with a loose knot; repeat at other end. Cut the ribbon into two equal lengths and tie each one in a bow around the gathered fabric at each end, covering the casings.

Piped cushions

Cushion covers are one of the simplest soft furnishings to sew and one of the quickest ways to update an existing scheme – either by introducing a new colour or a new style. Piped or frilled, lace-edged or bordered, each finish will give a different character to a room.

First, decide on the cushions' function – are they just a decorative addition to a sofa or a bed, or will they need to be more practical, for example, to soften hard dining chairs, or to provide additional seating? The size and shape of the cushion depends on the answers to these questions.

Secondly, choose the fabric – match the cushion cover fabric to your other furnishings or go for a complete contrast of colour and pattern. Brighten up a neutral colour scheme with a riot of colourful covers or add just a subtle hint of colour with a paler hue taken from the main colour in the room.

Cushion pads and fillings

Nowadays it is easy to buy cushion pads in a range of shapes and sizes – square, rectangular and round, with or without gussets. You can choose the filling to suit your needs – most purchased cushion pads contain either a natural feather mixture or a synthetic filling such as polyester. A feather-filled pad will give a cushion that soft, inviting look and can be quickly plumped back into shape. Polyester filling is more practical as it is completely washable and is a must for people with allergies.

▼ **Piped perfection** *Piping made from a contrast colour picked from the cushion looks smart; made from the same fabric it gives a classic finish; while striped or checked fabric cut on the bias adds a jaunty touch.*

Adding piping

One of the simplest ways of transforming a plain cushion cover is with a line of piping round the outer edge. Piping will give the cushion a good outline, a professional finish and add strength to the seams. Decorative piping can be bought ready-made or you can make your own by covering a length of cord with a bias-cut fabric strip.

Piping cord comes in a range of thicknesses from 00 to 6; sizes 3 or 4 are the most suitable for decorative sofa cushions, but try to match the thickness to the size of the cushion. Take the covering fabric with you to the haberdashery department and wind it round the cord to gauge the effect. If you prefer a more prominent piping or have large cushions to edge, you can use a thick cord or a roll of wadding, which will give a fat piped edge. Traditionally, piping fabric covers the cord smoothly, but you can also gather the fabric, giving a slightly frilled edge to the cushion.

The covering strip is cut on the fabric bias – across the grain – so it will have enough 'give' to go round the cord and round the cover without puckering.

▼ *A neat finish* A piped trim is perfect for these formal cushions.

MAKING UP PIPING

1 Fabric quantities For the width of the covering strip, measure round the cord and allow an extra 2.5cm (1in) for seam allowances. For the length, measure round the cushion cover, allowing an extra 2cm (³/₄in) for joining.

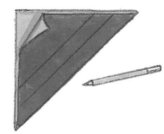

2 Cutting the bias strips Fold the fabric diagonally, so the cut edge lies along the selvedge. With your hand flat against the fabric fold, cut along the fold. Both diagonal edges are now cut along the fabric bias. Mark the required strip widths along the diagonal edges and cut out.

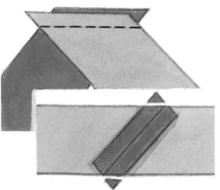

3 Joining strips together Fabric strips must be joined together on the straight grain. Place strips with right sides together; pin and stitch with a 6mm (¹/₄in) seam allowance. Press seam open. Trim off points.

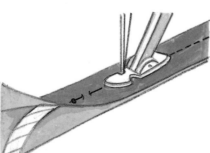

4 Covering the cord Fold the fabric strip in half round the cord with wrong sides together. Pin and stitch close to the cord using a zip foot attachment on the sewing machine to keep stitching close to the cord.

5 Joining piping To join piping together to fit round the cover, trim off both cord ends so they butt together. Bind over the ends to hold them firmly in place with sewing thread. Trim the covering fabric so one side overlaps the other for 2cm (³/₄in). Turn under 1cm (³/₈in) and place over raw edge. Pin and stitch over join.

Square cushions On a square cover, pin the covered piping to the right side of the top cover piece, with cut edges together and the stitching on piping 1.5cm (⁵/₈in) from the outer edge of the cover. At each corner, snip into piping fabric up to stitching. Using a zip foot, stitch along first side to the corner, work one stitch across corner and then stitch along next side. Repeat for the other two sides. If the fabric is thick, work two or three stitches diagonally across the corner to help cover to turn through the corners.

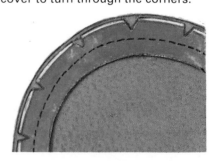

Round cushions On a round cover, place the covered piping to the cover in the same way as for square cover. Snip into the piping fabric up to stitching at about 2.5cm (1in) intervals, to help curve the piping round the edge. Stitch around piping using zip foot.

HOW TO MAKE GATHERED PIPING

1 Cutting fabric strips Measure the width of the piping fabric in the usual way. Measure round cushion and add ¹/₂-1 times extra for the length. Cut out the fabric strips on the bias in the usual way, joining to make the required length.

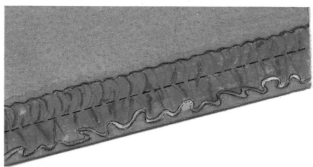

2 Gathering up the piping Fold the covering fabric in half round the cord and pin the cord to hold. Stitch for 15cm (6in) using the zip foot but do not stitch right up against the cord, as the tube needs to be loose enough to be gathered. Leaving the needle in the fabric, raise the pressure foot and gently pull the cord through the tube to gather up the fabric. Check the gathers are even, lower the foot and repeat, working in 15cm (6in) sections, until the end of the cord is reached.

3 Completing the cover Apply the gathered piping to a cover piece, joining the ends together in the same way as before. Stitch the gathered piping to the first cover piece, before adding the second cover section, checking the gathers are even as you work. Complete as for basic piped cover.

▼ *A gathered finish* A thick cord has been used in the piping to make a bold gathered edge to this attractive cushion. The fabric is a pretty glazed cotton with a floral pattern; the piping fabric is picked from one of the colours in the pattern.

MAKING A ZIPPED PIPED COVER

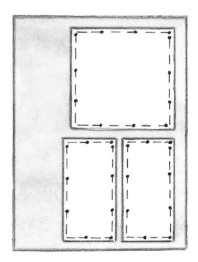

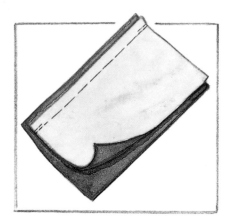

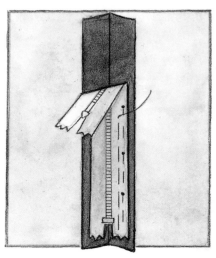

1 Cutting out Measure the cushion pad and cut a paper pattern to this size adding 1.5cm (⁵/₈in) all round for seams. Using the pattern, cut out one piece of fabric for the front. Fold and cut the pattern in half and pin the two halves to the fabric leaving 2.5cm (1in) between them. Cut out the back cover. Fold back cover in half and cut down fold to make two back pieces.

2 Joining the backs Place back pieces with right sides together; pin and tack a 1.5cm (⁵/₈in) seam. Stitch in from each end for 4cm (1¹/₂in), fastening off threads by back stitching for a short distance. Neaten edges of seam allowance by zigzag stitching or oversewing, then press seam open.

3 Inserting the zip Choose a zip 8cm (3in) smaller than centre back seam. Place zip right side down over wrong side of seam, matching teeth section of zip over tacked section of seam. Pin and tack in place. Using the zip foot, stitch zip in place. Remove tacking stitches.

4 Completing the cover Make up covered piping and set round front cover piece as described above. Place cover pieces with right sides together. Pin, tack and stitch all round cover, using zip foot to position stitches on, or just inside previous stitching line. Trim and neaten edges. Turn cover to right side through zip. Insert cushion pad and close zip.

◄ *Contrast edging* A shiny glazed cotton has been used for this piping. If you are using a patterned fabric, piping breaks up the edges of the cushion so that you don't have to match the design and can use up remnants of fabric economically.

Frilled cushions

Cushions, the most versatile of home furnishings, are synonymous with comfort, colour and style. Wherever they are placed, cushions have an immediate softening impact. Yet by trimming cushions in one of a variety of ways, they can be specially tailored to enhance individual rooms in your home.

Even the most basic frill can be adapted to different decorative styles. For example, a lace-frilled cushion brings frivolity and romance to a bedroom,

while a piped frill in a contrasting fabric adds a bold, cheerful finish to a cushion on a kitchen chair. Later chapters will cover more formal modifications of the cushion frill – pleated frills, for example.

The simplest frills are made from a single layer of fabric with a neatened outer edge. They can be bound with a contrast edging, finished with a double hem, or with decorative machine stitching such as closely worked zigzag stitch, or one of the attractive edge

▲ Piped and frilled
Insert the piping with the frill – the method used is the same for circular or square cushions.

stitches found on the newer machines.

A single frill produces a crisp finish while a double frill gives a fuller, softer edge. It is made from a folded strip of fabric and is stitched to the cover in the same way as a single frill.

15

MAKING A SINGLE-FRILLED COVER

1 Calculating the frill Measure round the cover and allow twice this for the frill length. The frill width is a matter of personal choice, but you will find that a frill wider than 7.5cm (3in) will be too floppy unless you are working with lace for bed cushions. Add an additional 3cm (1in) for double hem and seam allowance. Any extra needed for joining strips together should be included in the frill length.

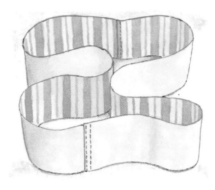

2 Cutting out the strips Cut the fabric strips on the straight of the grain – across the fabric width, from selvedge to selvedge. Working from the wrong side, using a metre stick and tailor's chalk or marking pencil, measure and mark the strips across the fabric. Cut out carefully along the marked lines.

3 Joining the strips together The frill strips must be joined together into a ring to fit round the front cushion cover piece. Pin and stitch the frill strips together with narrow French seams (see page 85). If the pattern is distinctive, try to match the designs over the seam.

4 Hemming the frill Turn under 1cm ($^3/_8$in) all round the outer edge of frill. Turn under another 1cm ($^3/_8$in), forming a double hem. Pin and tack hem in place. Either machine stitch or hem the frill by hand with small invisible stitches.

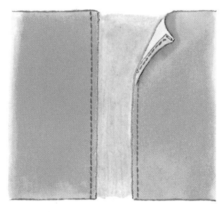

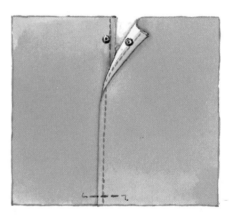

6 Stitching frill to front cover Cut out one cover piece in the same way as for piped cushions (see page 14). With right sides together and raw edges matching, pull up gathering stitches to fit round the cushion cover and pin. Check that the gathers are evenly spaced. On square covers it may be necessary to allow extra gathers to go round each corner. Tack and stitch the frill to the cover.

7 Making a non-fastening back opening Fold paper pattern in half and cut as for piped cushions. Place pattern on fabric and cut out, adding 6cm (2in) to both centre edges. Turn under and stitch a double 1cm ($^3/_8$in) hem along both centre edges.

8 Completing back cover To keep opening taut after pad is inserted add press studs or velcro to the opening. With right sides up, overlap the hemmed edges for 4cm (1$^1/_2$in) and attach fastening; then pin and tack together along outer seamlines.

▶ *Double up with lace*
Purchased lace, slightly narrower than the frill, can be added for a softer finish. Pin the lace to the frill after it has been hemmed but before gathering. There are so many different designs of lace – soft and romantic, bold and chunky – so choose a style to suit the furnishings in the room.

5 **Gathering the frill** Work two rows of gathering stitches along the length of the frill.

9 **Finishing off** Place back to front with right sides together, sandwiching the frill. Pin and stitch together all round, making sure that the stitching matches or is worked inside the previous line of stitching. Trim seam to reduce bulk of gathering and turn cover right side out. Insert the cushion pad through back opening.

▲ *Piped detail* *Taking a lead from the upholstery, this pair of cushions shows two variations of piped and frilled finishes. A length of covered piping cord can be inserted between the frill and the cover. Make up the* *piping and tack round the front cover before adding the frill. The fabric is quite stiff so hemmed single frills have been used with the one-sided printed fabric backed with the reversible plain.*

Perfect gathering

Heavy fabric If your chosen fabric is medium to heavy weight, the long gathering threads may break when they are pulled up. Stitch the gathering rows in short sections and position the rows on either side of any seams. It is difficult to pull gathering threads through the seam thickness.

Frill fullness When gauging the amount of fullness in a frill, take account of the fabric's weight. For a thick fabric that gathers more bulkily than the standard-weight furnishing cotton, one-and-a-half times the length will be sufficient, while for very fine fabrics, such as lawn, you may need two to three times the measurement.

A contrasting edge Single frills can be finished with a bound edge using contrasting ribbon, tape or bias binding. Fold binding in half over the raw frill edge and machine stitch in place. For a wider edging, hem the frill then place the binding on the edge and stitch along both sides.

MAKING A DOUBLE FRILL

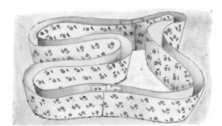

Making the frill A double frill is a folded strip of fabric which does not need a finished edge. If the fabric used is firmly woven, a double frill may need extra give. In this case cut the strips on the bias of the fabric (see page 12). Decide on the frill depth and length and cut out strips to twice this depth plus twice the seam allowance, by the chosen length, as for single frills.

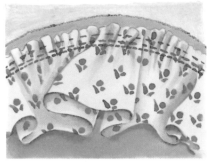

Adding the double frill to a cover
Join strips together into a ring with plain flat seams; trim and press open. Fold strip in half lengthways, wrong sides together; pin raw edges together and press along fold. Gather up through both layers and stitch to cover as for single frills.

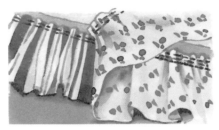

Working with more than one frill
Make up two or more frills in the same way as for single frills, making each one slightly smaller in size – about 2cm (³/₄in). Match the raw edges together and gather up as for a single fabric.

▼ *Doubling up*
A double frill is ideal for reversible cushions.

Beautiful bolsters

L ong, firm bolster cushions fit easily into any decor. Traditionally used at each end of a sofa or to provide a prop for other pillows on a bed, they can also be used to transform a bed into a sofa or as a support on window seats, easy chairs or sofas.

If you already have a bolster cushion you can re-cover this, or buy a bolster-shaped cushion pad to the size you require. These only come in a limited range of sizes, however, but you can make your own quickly and economically by cutting about 1m (1yd) of wadding as wide as the length of the bolster and rolling it into a pad. Sew the end in place with loose slipstitches to hold, then make a cover to fit.

▲ Plain and simple
On a tailored sofa where the other cushions are plain or with a flange, a simple bolster with piped seams at each end is perfectly in keeping with the style.

Materials

Bolster pad or 1m (1yd) **wadding (batting)** made into a pad.
Matching **zip** 6cm (2¼in) shorter than the bolster.
Matching **sewing thread**.
Optional **piping** and other trimmings.
Lining or remnant for the bolster with gathered ends.

HOW TO MAKE A PLAIN BOLSTER

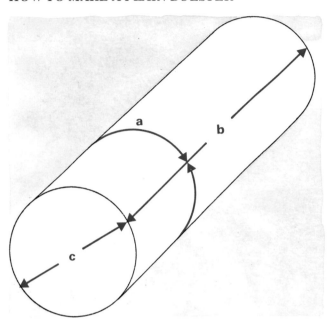

1 Cutting out Measure round the bolster to find its circumference (a) – measure loosely so that the cover will have an easy fit. Cut a piece of fabric this measurement plus 3cm (1¼in) by the length of the bolster (b) plus 3cm (1¼in). Measure across the end of the bolster (c) and cut two circles this measurement plus 3cm (1¼in) across.

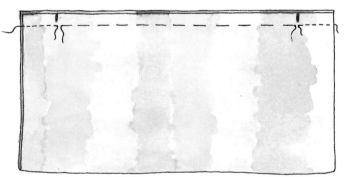

2 Stitching the main piece Place the zip centrally along one lengthways edge of the rectangle and mark each end on the fabric with tailor's chalk. Fold the fabric lengthways, right sides together and with edges matching, then machine stitch the ends of the seam past the marks, taking a 1.5cm (⅝in) seam allowance. Tack the remainder of the seam together.

3 Inserting the zip Insert the zip, centred in the seam as for square cushion, (see page 14). Remove the tacking.

(see page 14)

▶ *Daydream*
On a pretty day-bed, the bolsters give support to the cushions to make it look more like a sofa. The gathers on the ends of the bolsters fit in beautifully with the other frilled cushions used.

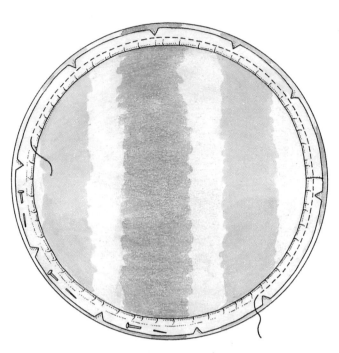

4 Attaching the piping Make up enough covered piping cord to go round the two circular end pieces (see page 12). Snip into the seam allowance of the bias strip used to cover the cord at 2.5cm (1in) intervals for ease and stitch to each end piece with seamlines matching, using a machine zip foot.

5 Attaching the end pieces At each end of the main piece, snip into the 1.5cm (⅝in) seam allowance at 2.5cm (1in) intervals for ease. Then, with right sides together, pin, tack and stitch a circular piece to each end of the main piece. Turn right side out through the zip opening and insert the pad. Close zip.

BOLSTER WITH GATHERED ENDS

1 Cutting out Cut out the main piece and insert the zip as in steps 1-3 for a plain bolster. Cut out a circle for each end from lining fabric as in step 1. Cut two strips of fabric one and a half times the circumference of the bolster, with a width half the measurement across the end plus 1.5cm (⅝in).

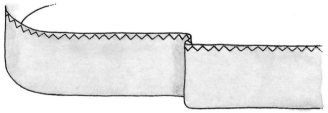

2 Making the gathered ends Neaten one raw edge of each strip of fabric with tight zigzag or overlock. If fabric frays badly, turn a narrow 5mm (¼in) hem. Fold each strip in half widthways, with right sides facing, and stitch the ends together to make a ring, taking a 1.5cm (⅝in) seam allowance. Press the seam allowances open.

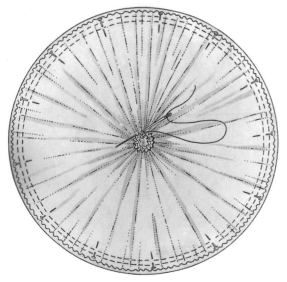

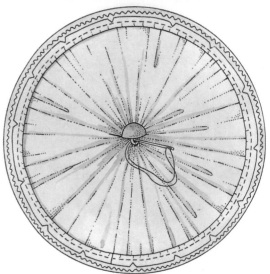

3 **Gathering up** Run two rows of gathering threads close to each long edge of each strip. Gather up the unfinished edge to fit the outside edge of each circle of lining fabric; pin. Pull up the other gathering threads tightly so that the fabric lies flat on the circle; pin. Tack the gathered fabric, right side up, to the right side of each circle round the edge and at the centre. Remove the gathering threads.

4 **Finishing off** Stitch the piping to the end pieces, as in step 4 for the plain bolster, stitch the fabric in place at the centre, then remove the tacking. Cover a large button with fabric and stitch to the centre of each end to cover the meeting edges of the gathered fabric. Attach the ends to the main piece as in step 5, for the simple bolster.

BOLSTER PILLOW

The soft, feminine styling of this type of bolster cover makes it particularly appropriate for the bedroom. It is quick and easy to make since it is gathered in at each end with a ribbon or length of coloured cord instead of having a zip fastening.

Buy or make the bolster the width of a pillow or long enough to go across the whole bed. Each cover also requires 1.5m (1½yd) of 6mm (¼in) ribbon or cord.

1 Cutting out Measure across one end of the bolster and along the length; add 5cm (2in) for the length of the fabric required. For the width, loosely measure round the circumference of the bolster and add 3cm (1¼in). Cut out one piece of fabric this size.

2 Making the casings Fold under 1cm (⅜in) then 1.5cm (⅝in) at each end to form casings for the ribbon or cord. Pin and then edgestitch close to the hem fold.

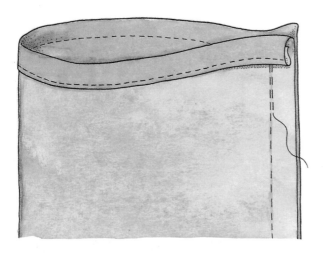

3 Stitching the seam Fold the fabric in half lengthways, with right sides together and edges matching. Pin and then stitch raw edges together taking a 1.5cm (⅝in) seam allowance and leaving casings free at ends. Backstitch at each end for strength.

▲ Fancy that
For the bed, the softer look of gently gathered bolster covers is ideal. Add a lace trimming to the edge for that little bit extra.

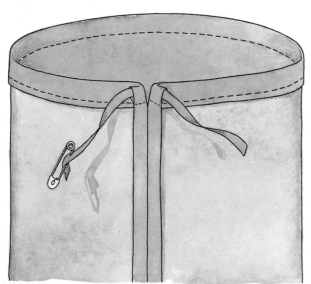

tip

Bolster pillow variation

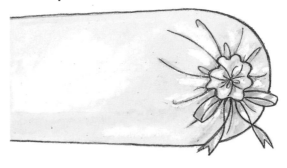

Cut the fabric 3cm (1¼in) wider than the circumference of the pillow by the length of the pillow plus 12cm (4¾in). Fold in half lengthways, right sides together and stitch a 1.5cm (⅝in) seam to form a tube. Hem each end, turning under 5mm (¼in) and then 1.5cm (⅝in). Insert the bolster pillow centrally and tie 80cm (⅞yd) ribbon round the fabric at each end like a Christmas cracker. Tie the ribbon in a bow and trim the ends at an angle for a neat finish.

4 Finishing off Cut the ribbon or cord in half and use a safety pin to thread a piece through the casing at each end. Turn the bolster cover through to the right side; draw up one end with the ribbon and tie in a bow, then trim the ribbon ends at an angle. Insert the pad and then draw up the other end and tie.

Buttoned cushions

Buttoning gives gusseted cushions the appearance of over-stuffed luxury, making the cushions look deeper and therefore more comfortable. The buttons, which are usually covered with fabric, can be added to most types of cushions, from simple scatter cushions to deep gusseted chair seats. They are not advisable for very thin squab cushions, however, since the buttons will not sink deep into the pad, making them uncomfortable to sit on.

The idea for buttoning came into popularity in Victorian times, when buttons were widely used on all types of furniture from foot stools to Chesterfield sofas. Perhaps, because of this, buttoned cushions and furniture have an old-fashioned look which is now very much back in style.

Fabric covered buttons

Most buttoning is done with covered buttons, which look and feel softer than ordinary dressmaking buttons. The special buttons used for this can be either plastic or rust-proof metal, but although plastic is fine for dressmaking purposes, the strong metal variety is best for cushions.

Any light or mediumweight fabric can be used to cover the buttons, and you may have some remnants of attractive fabric already, which would be ideal for the purpose. Usually all the buttons are covered with the same fabric, but for added interest you could use a different colour for each one to create a harlequin effect. You can even embroider fabric or use stitched canvas as the button covers.

▼ Springtime
Buttoning makes deep cushions look invitingly plump, soft and springy. Here the buttons are covered with bias binding which was used to trim the piping giving a springtime look.

COVERING METAL BUTTONS

1 Cutting the pattern Buy medium to large cover buttons for cushion buttoning – between 19 and 29mm (¾ and 1¼in). Cut out the circle on the back of the pack which is the correct size for the buttons you are covering. This is your pattern.

2 Cutting the fabric Position the pattern on the right side of the fabric and move it around so that the pattern covers a motif. If the motifs are too large for this, decide on the colour you would like to highlight, and position the pattern accordingly. Draw round the pattern and then cut out the fabric; repeat for all the buttons you wish to cover.

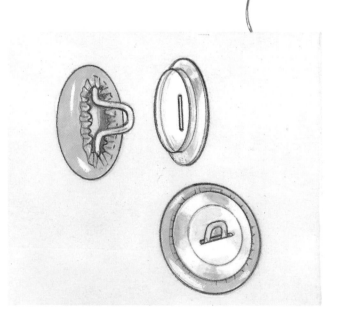

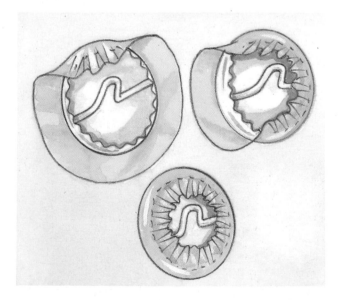

3 Covering the top Position the fabric circles wrong side up. Separate the two parts of a button and centre the larger, top half upside down on a fabric circle. Ease the fabric over the button, pressing it down on to the small teeth around the button rim. Use a pin to press the fabric into place, if necessary.

4 Assembling the button Check that the fabric is smooth on the top part of the button. If so, quickly press the hollow side of the bottom part on to the stem of the button; it should snap together with the top part, neatly covering the raw edges of the fabric. Cover the remaining buttons in the same way.

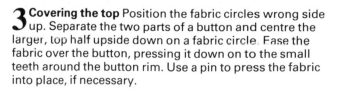

► *Button focus*
The front of this pretty pillow is made in four triangular sections, trimmed with double-edged lace and then stitched together. The button is the finishing touch, focusing attention on construction of the pillow, and covering the point where the four triangles meet.

COVERING PLASTIC BUTTONS

Unlike metal buttons, plastic ones do not have teeth to secure the fabric, which means that they are covered in a slightly different way.

1 Cutting out Cut out circles of fabric using the appropriate pattern on the back of the pack of cover buttons as in steps 1 and 2 opposite.

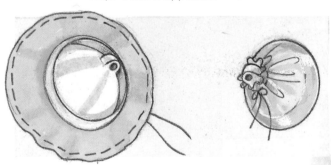

2 Covering the top Run a row of gathering stitches close to the edge of a fabric circle, with the two thread ends pulled out on the right side. Separate the two halves of each button, and position the top part upside down on the wrong side of the fabric. Pull up the thread ends to gather the fabric, and tie in a knot close to the button stem. Trim off the thread ends.

3 Assembling the button Check that the fabric is smooth on the top part of the button and then press the hollow side of the bottom piece on to the button stem; it should snap together with the top piece, neatly covering the fabric edges. Cover the remaining buttons in the same way.

tip

Spare parts
Manufacturers usually supply an extra button on ready-made garments in case a button is lost. For the same reason, its a good idea to cover an extra button when making buttoned cushions, and keep it safely in reserve.

Materials

Covered cushion
Large covered **buttons**
Furnishing fabric
Button twine, available from the sewing departments of some of the larger chain stores or from specialist upholstery suppliers. It comes in only a few colours, but it will not show on the finished cushion, so an exact match is not necessary.

BUTTONING CUSHIONS

1 Planning For each button on the front of the cushion you will need another one on the back for reinforcement. This can either be a small, inexpensive button, or, if the cushion is reversible, a second covered button. Use tailor's chalk to mark the position of the buttons on each side, making sure that the button marks on the underside are exactly under the ones on the top.

2 Attaching the buttons Thread a needle with button twine and knot the ends together to make a double thread. Pass the needle from the underside of the cushion to the top, making sure the needle goes through the marks on both sides. Thread on a button and stitch back to the underside. Thread on another button and stitch to the top side and through the top button.

3 Knotting off Pull firmly on the twine to tighten the thread and pull the two buttons into the cushion. Pass the twine round the shank of the button to make a loop and then pass the needle through the loop to secure the buttons.

4 Finishing off Tie another knot in the thread, then trim. Repeat steps 2-4 to attach all the required buttons, pulling them the same depth into the cushion.

▲ Comfort first
Buttons add decorative interest to squab cushions, but make sure the cushions are deep enough to allow the buttons to sink in, otherwise they may be uncomfortable to sit on.

Gusseted cushions

Adding a gusset to a cushion cover allows for a deeper, more tailored shape. The gusset strip forms the side between the top and bottom pieces of the cover. The three dimensional shape produced can be emphasized by piping the seams or with a decorative or contrasting gusset. Gusseted cushions can be square, rectangular or round and used on hard chairs, benches or sofas.

The zip is inserted in the back part of the gusset where it will not be seen. The zip usually extends round the sides of the cushion to make it easier to insert the pad or foam. This is especially important if the foam is very firm. The length of the extension will largely depend on the thickness of the foam or pad - the deeper the cushion, the longer the extension each side.

▲ **Terrace seating**
Provençal fabric, in bright colourways, has been used to make a set of cheerful cushions for folding wooden chairs. As the gusset is quite narrow it is made from a single strip of fabric with the zip inserted along the seamed edge, just under the piping.

Choosing the pads

The type of filling you should choose depends on whether you want a firm or soft cushion. For a firm cushion which retains its shape and looks neat, choose block foam. It's easy to use, resilient and washable. The thickness of the foam depends on where the cushion is to be used – seat cushions are usually about 10cm (4in) thick.

If you prefer a softer look, choose a loose filling – feathers, feathers and down, or foam chips. Feathers and down are a luxurious filling, but their extreme softness means that they should only be used for thick gusseted cushions. When using loose fillings, the filling is stuffed into an inner cover. This enables you to remove the outer cover for washing.

Suitable fabrics

This type of cushion will usually get a lot of wear, so choose closely woven, washable fabrics for the cover; furnishing fabrics such as heavy cotton, corduroy, glazed cottons or linen are ideal.

 ► A perfect fit
This deep, gusseted cushion fits neatly into the seat of a cane armchair. The washable cotton fabric used matches the wallpaper, and a simple squab cushion with ties adds comfort to the back.

MAKING A GUSSETED CUSHION

1 Making the filling If using block foam, buy or cut it to the correct size. For loose fillings, make an inner cover from downproof cambric in the same way as the outer cover, but omitting the zip, and stuff with the filling.

2 The outer cover Measure the width and length of the top of the foam or soft-filled pad and add 3cm (1¼in) to both measurements for seam allowances. Cut two pieces of fabric this size.

3 Measuring the gusset The gusset is made up of two pieces: the front and sides are cut as one, while the back piece, in which the zip is inserted, is cut separately. Measure the front gusset - the depth of the pad by three quarters of each of the two sides, plus the length of the front. Add standard 1.5cm (⅝in) seam allowances all round.

Measure the back gusset - the depth of the pad by a quarter of each of the two sides plus the length of the back. For seam allowances add 3cm (1¼in) to the length and 6cm (2½in) to the width. Cut two lengths of fabric to these dimensions.

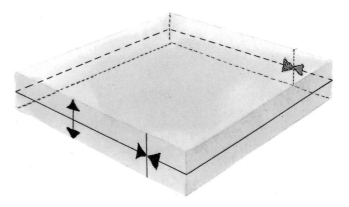

◄ An inviting corner
This window seat, made from a single cushion, is just the place to curl up with your favourite magazine. The feather pad has been shaped with the sides angled outwards to fit the area snugly.

tip

Tailored look
For a tailored effect, make the gusset in four pieces instead of two, with seams at each front corner. This requires accurate measuring, cutting and stitching to ensure that the seams are straight and positioned exactly at corners.

When joining gusset pieces together, leave 1.5cm (⅝in) free at each end. The fabric will spread at the corners to aid stitching the gusset to the top and base pieces.

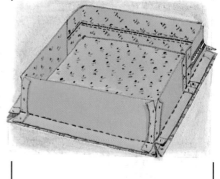

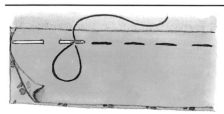

4 Inserting the zip The zip should be 3cm (1¼in) shorter than the back gusset section. Cut the back gusset in half lengthways. Place right sides together; pin and tack down the complete length. Press seam open.

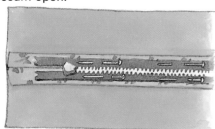

5 Position zip centrally Place zip face down over wrong side of seam. Pin and tack in place. Turn to right side; stitch zip in place.

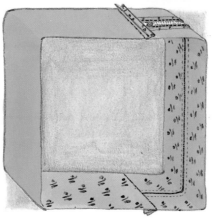

6 Making up the gusset With right sides facing and taking 1.5cm (⅝in) seam allowances, pin the ends of gusset pieces together. Check for fit round cushion pad, then stitch seams.

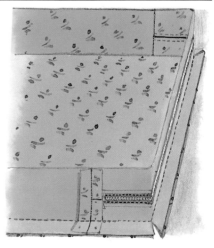

7 Stitching gusset to main pieces With right sides facing, pin and tack one edge of the gusset to one cushion piece. Snip into gusset at corners to help the fabric lie flat. Open the zip, then stitch second cover piece to opposite edge of gusset in the same way. For a crisp look, add contrast piping to these seams (see pages 11-14). Turn right side out and insert pad; close zip.

29

ROUND GUSSETED COVERS

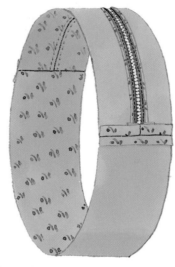

1 Make a pattern Pin a piece of paper on the chair, and draw round the seat area to make a circular pattern. If you are using a circular foam pad, draw round this instead. Fold into four to check it is symmetrical and trim if necessary. Add seam allowances all round.

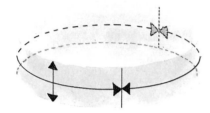

2 Measuring the gusset The gusset is cut in two pieces, like a square or rectangular cushion. Measure up in the same way so that the back gusset extends about a third of the way round the cushion. Add seam allowances as in step 3 of making a gusseted cushion.

3 Inserting the zip Cut the back gusset in half lengthways. Insert the zip in the same way as for square or rectangular cover. With right sides facing and taking 1.5cm (⁵⁄₈in) seam allowance, pin and stitch gusset pieces together along short edges.

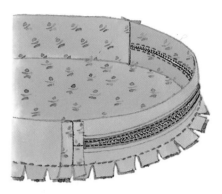

4 Stitching gusset to main cover With zip open and right sides facing, pin and stitch the gusset to one cover piece and then the other. Snip into seam allowances at 2.5cm (1in) intervals all round, to ease the fabric and achieve a neat appearance. Turn cover right side out. Insert pad; close zip.

tip

Concealing the zip
If the gusset can be seen all the way round when the cushion is in position, re-position the zip where it will be less conspicuous. The easiest method is to put the zip on the underside, as in a squab cushion, although this means you cannot turn the cushion over. On a thin, square cushion it can also be positioned on the back gusset in the seam, but the zip should not extend round the corners.

◀ *Formal comfort*
Deep, gusseted cushions provide comfort on this wicker sofa. The large print has been cleverly matched on the top and front gusset for a professional finish. The seams are subtly piped in green.

Tucked cushions

By stitching lines of folds into a plain fabric, you can add surface detail and create a whole range of innovative designs. The tucks are machine stitched either horizontally or vertically along the grain of the fabric, and can vary in width and spacing according to the chosen pattern or personal preference.

Elaborate tucked designs can be shown off to the full on cushion covers, like those shown here, but the technique can also be used to add a simple decorative trimming to the edges of pillowcases, tablecloths and napkins.

Suitable fabrics
Plain fabrics in light shades are best for displaying tucks, as they will allow the eye to focus on the tucked design, rather than on the fabric pattern. Elaborate patterns also become distorted by tucks and can look odd, though with careful planning, simple checks and stripes can produce wonderful results. Check the effect by pleating your chosen fabric into a series of small folds before you buy.

Your chosen fabric should be evenly and closely woven, making it easier for you to ensure that the tucks are accurately folded and stitched along the grain; always cut the fabric along the grain. For the best results, choose a fabric that presses into a sharp crease line, and avoid slippery fabrics which are difficult to work with, like satin and many synthetics. When selecting a fabric, also bear in mind that each tuck takes up three times as much fabric as its

▲ A tuck in time
The beauty of these tucked cushions lies in the simplicity of their designs, which are created from the addition of textured surface detail. Use plain, lightweight fabrics for the best results, and make the cushions in a range of colours.

finished width, so try and choose a reasonably priced fabric, particularly if your design incorporates several tucks.

Lawn or lightweight cotton and linen are ideal. Furthermore, if you use fine fabrics like these, the triple layer of fabric made by each tuck will create strong bands of colour against untucked areas of the cushion, and greatly enhance the overall design.

Materials

Note: The metric to imperial measurements are not exact conversions, but have been calculated so the cushions are easy to make. Follow only one set of figures.

Lemon yellow fabric for the yellow cushion: you will need a piece 91 × 43cm (34¾ × 17in) for the front of the cushion, and 46 × 43cm (18 × 17in) for the back

Pale blue fabric for the blue cushion: you will need a 67cm (25¼in) square for the front of the cushion, and a piece 46 × 43cm (18 × 17in) for the back

Ivory fabric for the ivory cushion: you will need two rectangles of fabric for the front. Piece A – 171 × 31cm (66½ × 11¾in), and Piece B – 87 × 59cm (35 × 23in), plus one piece for the back, 46 × 43cm (18 × 17in)

Pale pink fabric for the ruffle tuck cushion: you will need a piece 119 × 43cm (47 × 17in) for the front of the cushion, and 46 × 43cm (18 × 17in) for the back

Dark pink fabric for the irregularly tucked cushion; calculate the fabric requirements from your design: our cushion was made from a piece 83 × 43 cm (33 × 17in) for the front, and 46 × 43cm (18 × 17in) for the back

Zip 35cm (13¾in) long for each cushion, to match the fabric

Matching sewing threads

Tailor's chalk

Ruler

Square cushion pad 40cm (15¾in) for each cushion

Iron and **pressing cloth**

YELLOW CUSHION

This cushion has a design of regular tucks, each of which is 2cm (¾in) wide from the fold to the stitching line. The tucks are arranged in three bands – two outer bands of three tucks, and one central band of six tucks, with spaces of untucked fabric in-between.

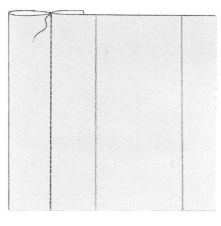

1 Marking a seam allowance Lay out the fabric for the front cover, right side face up. Use tailor's chalk to mark a 1.5cm (⅝) seam allowance along one short edge.

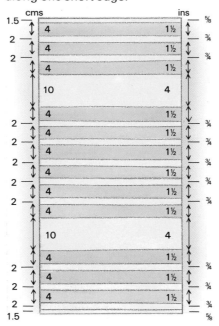

cms			ins	
1.5				⅝
2	4	1½		¾
2	4	1½		¾
	4	1½		¾
	10	4		
2	4	1½		¾
2	4	1½		¾
2	4	1½		¾
2	4	1½		¾
2	4	1½		¾
	4	1½		¾
	10	4		
2	4	1½		¾
2	4	1½		¾
2	4	1½		¾
1.5				⅝

2 Marking the tucks Using either centimetres or inches, work from the diagram, to mark up the stitching lines. Measure and mark the tuck widths down both sides of the fabric, using tailors chalk, then join them with chalked lines ruled across the fabric, finishing with a 1.5cm (⅝in) seam allowance; the shaded areas indicate the pleats.

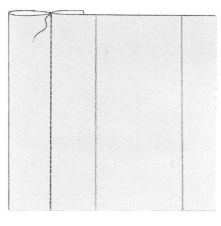

3 Stitching the tucks Starting with the first tuck, fold the fabric wrong sides together, matching the two stitching lines. Tack and then machine along the stitching line. Repeat for the rest of the tucks.

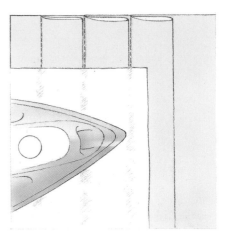

4 Pressing the tucks Use a slightly damp pressing cloth to press the tucks along their folds; this will give a sharp edge, without adding shine or scorching the fabric. Then press the tucks flat, so that they all lie in the same direction.

5 Making the zip opening Cut a 43 × 6cm (17 × 2¼in) strip of fabric from the back cover fabric. With right sides together and long edges matching, pin and tack the strip back on to the main back piece, taking a 1.5cm (⅝in) seam allowance; machine stitch the seam for 4cm (1½in) only at each end, leaving the centre tacked together. Press the seam flat along its whole length.

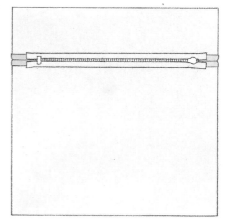

6 Inserting the zip Lay the zip right side down over the wrong side of the cushion back, with the teeth directly over the seam. Tack then machine stitch the zip in place. Remove tacking.

7 Joining front to back With right sides together, pin and stitch the back cover to the front around all four sides, taking a 1.5cm (⅝in) seam allowance. Trim diagonally across each corner, then turn cover through to right side via the zip opening. Press the seams.

IVORY CUSHION

This cushion is made from two triangles of tucked fabric, stitched together on the diagonal to form a square cover. On one fabric triangle (Piece A), the tucks are shorter and stop at the diagonal seam; on the other (Piece B), the tucks extend right across the cushion's diagonal, from one edge to the other. All the finished tucks are 2cm (¾in) wide.

1 Making the tucks on Piece A Lay out the 171 × 31cm (66½ × 11¾in) rectangle of fabric with right side up, and mark a 1.5cm (⅝in) seam allowance across one of the short edges. Mark a series of tucks 4cm (1½in) wide, interspersed with gaps of 2cm (¾in) along the length – ie 4cm (1½in), 2cm (¾in), 4cm (1½in), 2cm (¾in), etc. This will give you 28 tucks (or 29 if using inches), ending with a 2cm (¾in) space, plus a 1.5cm (⅝in) seam allowance. Stitch the tucks as before, then press them flat.

2 Making the tucks on Piece B Lay out the 87 × 59cm (35 × 23in) rectangle of fabric, right side up, and mark a 1.5cm (⅝in) seam allowance along the short edge. Mark the stitching lines as for piece A to make 14 tucks (or 15 if using inches) across the fabric. Stitch the tucks, and press to lie flat.

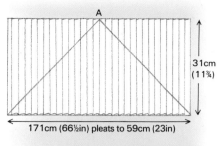

A

171cm (66½in) pleats to 59cm (23in)

31cm (11¾)

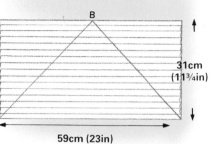

B

31cm (11¾in)

59cm (23in)

3 Trimming to form triangles The fabric rectangles are trimmed to make two triangles. Measure halfway across the long side of Piece A, which should now measure 59cm (23in). Mark two lines from this point down to the two bottom corners of the rectangle, and trim the excess away to make a triangle. Repeat on Piece B, whose long side also measures 59cm (23in); note that the tucks lie horizontally, not vertically.

4 Joining the triangles With right sides together and longest edges matching, pin then stitch the two triangles together along the longest edge to form a square, taking a 1.5cm (⅝in) seam allowance. Make up as for the yellow cushion.

tip

Ivory cushion short cut
Once confident with tucking, save on time and fabric when making the ivory cushion by working from two triangles of fabric at the start, rather than two rectangles which then need to be trimmed.

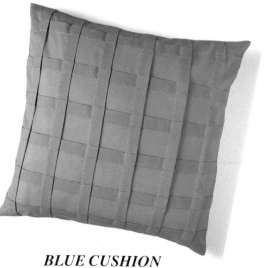

BLUE CUSHION

Stunning chequered designs can also be created by stitching lines of vertical, as well as horizontal tucks. This design has six vertical and six horizontal 2cm (¾in) tucks, with 4cm (1½in) squares of untucked fabric in-between.

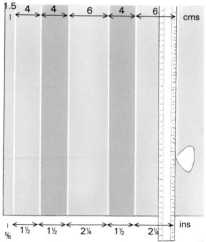

1.5 | 4 | 4 | 6 | 4 | 6 | cms

⅝ | 1½ | 1½ | 2¼ | 1½ | 2¼ | ins

1 Making the horizontal tucks With right side up, mark a 1.5cm (⅝in) seam allowance along one edge of the front cover fabric. Then mark up the design. Begin with the first 4cm (1½in) space, then measure 4cm (1½in) for the first tuck; leave a 6cm (2¼in) space before marking 4cm (1¼in) for the next tuck. Continue marking up 6cm (2¼in) spaces and 4cm (1½in) tucks (shaded in the diagram), ending with a 6cm (2¼in) space and a 1.5cm (⅝in) seam allowance. Stitch the tucks, and press.

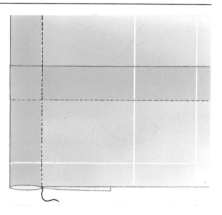

2 Making the vertical tucks Turn the fabric so that the tucks lie horizontally. Mark up the vertical tucks exactly as for the horizontal ones. When stitching the vertical tucks, carefully fold and stitch across the horizontal tucks as you go. Press flat with a slightly damp pressing cloth. Make up as for the yellow cushion.

◄ *Matching set*
Make co-ordinated cushions in various shades of the same colour.

2 Making the tucks Mark up the stitching lines for the 4cm (1½in) tucks, with 2cm (¾in) gaps in-between, as for the ivory cushion. This will give you 19 tucks (or 20 if using inches), finishing with a 2cm (¾in) space, plus a 1.5cm (⅝in) allowance. Stitch and press tucks.

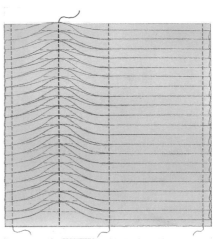

PALE PINK CUSHION

Ruffle tucks look stunning, and are suprisingly easy to stitch. Experiment with this technique on fine, silk-like fabrics which catch the light for a striking two-tone effect. On the cushion all the finished tucks are 2cm (¾in) wide.

1 Getting started With right side face up, use tailor's chalk to mark a 1.5cm (⅝in) seam allowance along one short edge of the front cover fabric, followed by a 2cm (¾in) gap, before marking the first tuck.

3 Creating a ruffled effect Lay out the fabric so that the tucks lie horizontally and face away from you. Tack and stitch down both sides of the cushion front, 1.5cm (⅝in) in from the side edges, and also down the cushion centre, so that the tucks are stitched to lie flat. Turn the fabric around so that the tucks face you. Measure halfway between two rows of stitching and tack and stitch the tucks to lie flat in the opposite direction (a); repeat between the other two rows of stitching. Make up as for the yellow cushion.

DARK PINK CUSHION

Many attractive designs can be made using different sized tucks and spaces. For a symmetrical look carefully plan your design before you begin, or make a more random pattern by inventing it as you go.

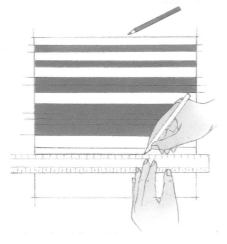

1 Planning a design If planning a design, draw up a scaled-down diagram to work from, shading in the tucks for easy reference. In the design shown here, the tuck width varies from 1.5-2.5cm (⅝-1in).

2 Marking the tucks Lay out the front cover fabric with right side face up and mark a 1.5cm (⅝in) seam allowance along one short edge as usual. Carefully mark up the design from your drawing. You should always finish with a space for the last pressed tuck, plus a 1.5cm (⅝in) seam allowance.

3 Stitching and pressing Stitch the tucks and press them flat as before, so that they all lie in the same direction. Make up as for the yellow cushion.

Re-covering drop-in seats

A dining chair with a drop-in seat, can be smartened up or made to match new furnishings with a change of cover. Choose an elegant damask or needle-point fabric for a formal effect, or a pretty floral for something fresh. As long as the fabric is hard-wearing, any medium to heavyweight furnishing fabric can be used for the purpose.

Re-covering this type of chair need not be a major operation since the seat lifts out for easy handling, and it may be that only the top layer of fabric needs to

be replaced. Just 1m (1yd) of fabric or less will be enough to cover most chairs, and if the fabric has only a small or random pattern, this amount may be enough to cover two chairs.

Start by checking the state of the wood, and if necessary clean and re-finish it before you start on the fabric. Remove the outer layer of fabric, and if the layers underneath are in bad condition, remove them one by one until you get down to a sound layer.

▲ Quick recovery
A chair with a drop-in seat can be transformed with a new cover in a few hours. No sewing is necessary, and since all the work is done on the underside of the seat, it doesn't even have to be neat.

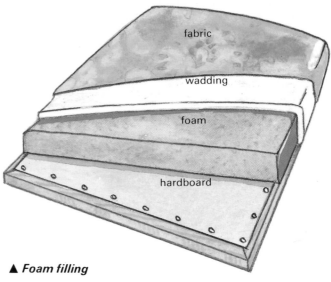

▲ *Foam filling*

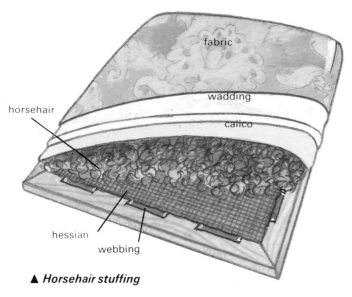

▲ *Horsehair stuffing*

Types of upholstery

The traditional drop-in seat comprises various layers of fabric and stuffing which give the seat its firm, but comfortable shape. Strips of strong webbing are stretched across the wooden seat frame in each direction to give the chair its base. A layer of hessian goes on top of this and then the horsehair or fibre mixture which makes up the main part of the seat. A layer of calico secures the horsehair and helps to prevent it working its way out. Cotton or polyester wadding on top of this add extra insulation for the horsehair and soften the overall effect, providing a smooth surface for the furnishing fabric which goes on top.

◄ *Pretty in chintz*
A floral chintz gives this chair a fresh but informal look, ideal for a cosy sitting room or kitchen.

Some modern chair seats are padded with foam which is placed on a hardboard or chipboard base and then covered with polyester or cotton wadding and then fabric. This is a quicker way of upholstering a seat, but not as durable or as comfortable as a traditionally upholstered seat.

Materials

Furnishing fabric of upholstery weight, 10cm (4in) larger all round than the fabric section of the chair seat.

An old **screwdriver** and a pair of **pincers** to remove old tacks or staples. A **tack** or **staple remover** will make this easier, but it is probably not worth buying one unless you plan to do several items.

Hammer and **16mm (⅝in) upholstery tacks** or a **staple gun** and **staples.** Staples are easy to use, but hard to take out. Professionals swear by tacks which can be partially nailed in for a temporary positioning and then knocked home when the arrangement has been finalized.

Fabric protector (optional).

If the layers underneath the main fabric are not in good condition, peel them apart to see what you need to replace. If the seat is upholstered with traditional materials, it may be necessary to replace the **wadding (batting)** and possibly also the **calico**, but it is unlikely that you will need to replace the remaining layers unless the chair is in very bad condition. If the chair is upholstered with **foam**, this can be replaced quite easily, especially since many suppliers will cut it to shape as part of their service.

RE-COVERING A DROP-IN SEAT

1 Removing the old fabric Push the seat up and out from underneath. Turn it upside down and remove the tacks or staples holding the fabric to the wooden frame. A staple or tack remover makes this easy, but tacks or staples can also be removed by carefully levering them up with a screwdriver and then pulling them out with pliers. If they are difficult to remove, try ripping off the fabric round them to make space underneath for the screwdriver. If a tack has lost its head, hammer the remains into the wood so that it does not catch on the new layers.

2 Arranging the fabric If the foam or wadding under the fabric is in good condition, all you need to do is replace the main fabric. Wrap the fabric loosely round the seat and stand back to survey the effect. If it has a large pattern or stripe, rearrange it to find the most pleasing effect. Always centre a large motif.

3 Temporary tacking With the lengthways grain running from front to back, and with the pattern arranged as required, place the fabric right side out on the chair seat and then turn the whole thing upside down. Knock a nail halfway into the wood at the centre of each edge as a temporary tack, with the fabric pulled taut. Alternatively fix a staple in these positions.

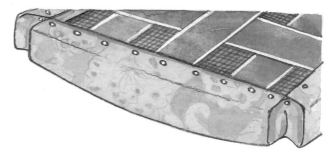

temporary tack

4 Tacking the edges Starting at the front of the seat, temporary tack or staple the fabric along the edge with the tacks spaced 4cm (1½in) apart. Tack the opposite edge and then the two side edges, pulling the fabric taut as you work, and leaving the corners free. When satisfied with the effect which should be smooth, hammer all the tacks home.

6 Finishing shaped corners Some chair seats have two corners with small square indents which accommodate the chair legs. Make a temporary tack in the centre as for a standard corner, pulling the fabric taut in the gap. Fold the excess fabric under to make pleats at each of the outer points and tack or staple in position; remove the temporary tack.

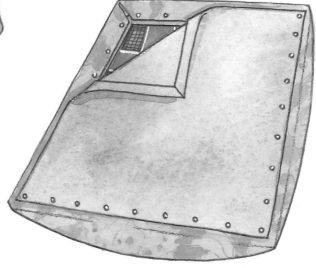

7 Neatening the underside If required, take a piece of spare fabric – hessian, calico, or lining fabric will do – and cut it 2.5cm (1in) larger all round than the frame. Turn under 3cm (1¼in) all round so that it is slightly smaller than the seat, and tack to the base of the frame to cover all the raw edges and to protect the stuffing layers from dust.

8 Preserving the fabric Once the seat has been re-covered, spray it with fabric protector to extend its life. Any marks which do get on the fabric should be removed with fabric dry-cleaning fluid.

Planning ahead
Tacks which are hammered deep into the chair frame are difficult to remove when it comes to re-covering the chair again. To make it easier to remove the fabric later, do not hammer the tacks completely flush with the fabric.

5 Finishing the corners Open out the fabric at the corners and hammer a temporary tack in the centre to hold (omit this stage if using staples). Fold the excess fabric on each side to the centre to make a pleat and tack or staple in place; remove the temporary tack.

Replacing the layers of padding

On a seat padded with foam, it may be worthwhile replacing the foam at the same time as the cover in order to extend the life of the seat and give it a fresh appearance.

On a seat traditionally upholstered with horsehair, it probably won't be necessary to replace all the layers unless the chair is in particularly bad condition. However, sometimes the wadding can wear thin and the horsehair starts to come through the calico, so these should both be replaced.

If the horsehair underneath the calico is in bad condition, it may be possible to top it up with new horsehair without completely renewing it; to renew the whole layer requires a bit more skill – this will be covered in a later chapter. Calico and wadding are widely available, but horsehair or its equivalent is available only from upholstery suppliers.

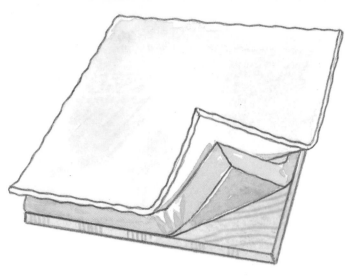

REPLACING FOAM

1 Measuring up Remove the old fabric and foam from the chair seat but leave the hardboard or chipboard in position. Draw round the seat on a piece of card to make a template for the new foam. Send the template to the foam supplier and get them to cut the foam to size.

2 Completing the seat Place the cut foam on the seat and cover with a piece of cotton or polyester wadding to soften the edges, 1cm (⅜in) larger all round (optional). Attach the fabric cover in the usual way (see previous pages).

▼ **Calico cover** A fresh calico cover keeps the horsehair stuffing underneath in place and provides a secure base for the wadding and main fabric cover.

REPLACING THE CALICO

Remove all the layers on the chair until you get down to the horsehair stuffing. Cut a new piece of calico to size and then fix to the chair in the same way as the main fabric, following the instructions on the previous pages but keeping the tacks well back from the inside edge where the tacks for the main fabric will go. If the frame is full of holes from previous tacks, the calico can be fixed to the sides of the frame instead, but make sure that the seat will still fit in the chair.

REPLACING THE WADDING

Traditionally cotton wadding is used on top of the calico to give the seat a soft, smooth finish, although 70g (2½oz) polyester wadding is an excellent alternative. Simply cut to the shape of the pad, adding 1cm (⅜in) all round to cover the sides of the seat. Position between the main fabric and the calico or foam and fix the main fabric on top, following the instructions on the previous pages.

Easy bedlinen

A duvet cover and pillowcases in fresh colours make the bed look bright and cheerful, and can invigorate the whole room. Made in fabrics with a white background, they look clean and cool for summer, while in rich, dark colours they look warm and luxurious.

By making the duvet cover and pillowcases yourself, you can choose exactly the fabrics you want to get just the right effect, and if you make the cover reversible, you will have two pattern options in one. Combine fabrics that tone in with the other fabrics used in

the room, or fabrics in the same colours, but with different patterns. Try a plain or striped fabric on one side, and florals or other country motifs on the other side.

To co-ordinate the pillowcases, make two sets – one to go with each side of the duvet cover. Alternatively, make the pillowcases from one fabric and trim with the other.

No complicated stitching is required to make either the duvet cover or the pillowcases, since all the seams are straight and hemming can be done on the machine. They shouldn't take you long

▲ Reverse to stripes
Stripes and florals are mixed together in this reversible duvet cover to provide two decorative options instead of one. The fabrics share the same colour and floral theme, making them co-ordinate well.

to make, either, and moreover the end results should be a lot more satisfying and will have cost you a lot less than ready-made versions.

Fabrics

Although still loosely called bed-linen, most sheets, pillowcases and duvet covers are now made from pure cotton or polyester-cotton. Pure linen and linen and cotton mixes are expensive and crease too easily to be popular for general use.

Polyester-cotton This is the most widely-used bedding fabric, being easy to wash and requiring little or no ironing. It can be bought in sheeting widths of 230cm (90in), which is wide enough for one side of a king-size duvet cover. Often manufacturers produce co-ordinated ranges of plain and patterned polyester-cotton sheeting, making it easy to mix and match.

Pure cotton This is a more luxurious fabric than polyester-cotton, and feels crisp and cool in summer. However it is more expensive than polyester-cotton, and you may find you need to join fabric widths across each side of a double or king-size duvet cover.

Duvet covers

Basically duvet covers are just large bags, sewn all round with a fastening in one short edge. Use whichever fastening you prefer – press fasteners or velcro are easiest, but you could use buttons or zip bought off the roll if preferred.

Sheeting fabrics can be used across the full width of each side, but narrow fabrics should be joined in the centre, with cut edges at the side. If your preferred fabric is expensive, make the duvet reversible, with a cheaper fabric on the underside. However, when mixing fabrics, always make sure they have the same fibre content, or they may shrink at different rates in the wash.

Estimating fabric requirements

Make the cover the same size as the duvet, so that the duvet fills it out completely to look plump and warm. Measure up and add 10cm (4in) to the length and 3cm (1¼in) to the width for seam and hem allowances. You will need

▲ Floral flair
Two co-ordinating floral fabrics in pinks and greens on a cream, background turn the bedroom into a riot of colour. One of the fabrics has a border pattern which has been cleverly used at the top end of the cover to give the effect of a sheet turned down. The fabric is used again to make a deep, flat bed valance.

two pieces this size – one in each fabric if making it reversible. Buy extra to match patterns.

To help estimate the fabric requirements and the length of fastening required, here are the standard duvet sizes, and the sizes that the openings should be in covers:

Single 140 × 200cm (55 × 78in). Make the opening 98cm (38½in) long.
Double 200 × 200cm (79 × 79in). Make the opening 148cm (58in) long.
King-size 220 × 230cm (86 × 90in). Make the opening 158cm (62in).

MAKING A REVERSIBLE DUVET COVER

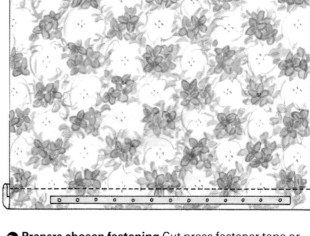

1 **Cut out and hem** Using the measurements given opposite, cut out two pieces of fabric the size of the duvet, adding 10cm (4in) to the length and 3cm (1¼in) to the width. This includes ease. On the bottom, short end of each piece, turn a double 2.5cm (1in) hem; pin and machine stitch.

2 **Prepare chosen fastening** Cut press fastener tape or velcro for the opening – 100cm (39in) long for a single duvet cover, 150cm (59in) for a double and 160cm (63in) for a king-size. Separate the two parts of the fastening, and pin one part to the right side of each piece of fabric, over the hem.

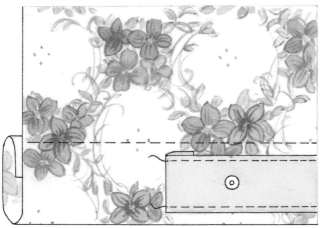

3 **Stitch the fastening** Place the two pieces together and check that the press fasteners correspond. Adjust if necessary. Turn under raw ends of press fastener tape and machine stitch down the long edges of each tape, using a zip foot. If using velcro, stitch along both long edges, without turning the ends under.

4 **Finish the opening edge** Place the pieces right sides together and join press fasteners or velcro. Tack from each side to 1cm (⅜in) past the tape, close to the hem edge. Stitch along the tacking, then at right angles across the hem and tape, as shown. Stitch twice for extra strength.

tip

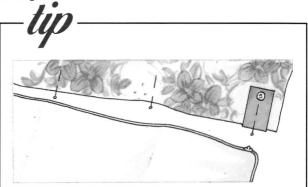

5 **Stitch french seams** With wrong sides together, stitch a 5mm (¼in) seam down both sides. Snip off corners. Turn wrong sides out, and stitch the seams again with a 1cm (⅜in) allowance to complete the french seams. Stitch remaining edge with a french seam in the same way. Turn cover right side out and press.

Prevent slipping
Prevent the duvet from slipping or from bunching at one end of the cover by using press fasteners. Cut a 6cm (2¼in) strip of ribbon, fold in half and stitch a press stud through both thicknesses near the folded end. Stitch the cover end of the ribbon to the corner of the cover. Sew the other half of the press stud to the corner of the duvet.

Pillowcases

New pillowcases give good results in the minimum of sewing time, and can be made to match either the sheet or the duvet cover. If you like to have two pillows, you can make the cover for the lower one to match the sheet, and the upper one to match the duvet.

Housewife pillowcases are the most straightforward to make and do not require a lot of fabric. Unlike duvet covers, there is no need for a complicated fastening – a flap inside the case is all you need to hold the pillow in place.

The pillowcase is cut in one piece, with one end folded over to form the flap which keeps the pillow in place, and the raw edges neatly enclosed in french seams.

As with all styles of pillowcase, a housewife pillowcase should fit the pillow loosely for a smooth effect. For this reason, when measuring up, add about 3cm (1¼in) to the length and width of the pillow for ease. Then add seam and hem allowances. A standard pillow is 75 x 50cm (29½ x 19¾in), so you will need a piece of fabric 174 x 56cm (68¾ x 22¼in) for each pillowcase.

▶ Inspired details
The question of how fancy to make an item is often determined by the fabric. Here, the pretty gathered frill on the top pillowcase perfectly complements the floral trellis design, while the more geometric combination of flowers and stripes, is better suited to the simple housewife style of pillowcase underneath.

SIMPLE HOUSEWIFE PILLOWCASE

1 Cut out and hem Cut a piece of fabric the same width as the pillow plus 6cm (2½in) by twice the length plus 24cm (9¾in). This includes ease. Stitch a double 1cm (⅜in) hem at one short end. At the other end turn under 5mm (¼in) and then 3.5cm (1½in) and stitch.

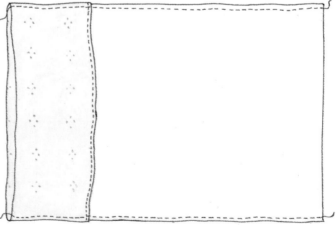

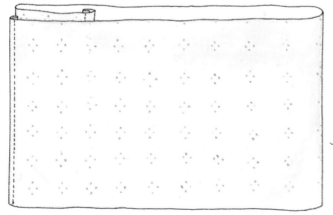

2 Form pocket flap At the end with the narrow hem, press 15cm (6in) to the wrong side to make the flap. Then fold the other end over so that it meets the fold of the flap and pin.

3 Stitch french seams Sew along long edges taking a 5mm (¼in) seam. Turn wrong sides out, press and stitch seams again taking 1cm (½in) seam allowance to complete the french seams. Turn right side out.

Frilled bedlinen

A frilled duvet cover and matching pillowcases are lovely additions to the bedroom, where their generous use of fabric adds a touch of luxury. The frills can be left plain and simple, or further embellished with ribbon, lace, binding or piping to add that extra personal detail.

On a pillow, the frill usually goes all the way round, although it can be placed only on the two short edges if preferred. On the duvet cover, however, it usually runs along the side and lower edges,

leaving the top edge free, where a frill might be irritating at night.

The frills can be either single or double, but if you want the duvet cover and pillowcases to be fully reversible, either bind the edges of the single frills or make double frills. Make the duvet cover from the same fabric on both sides, or with the frill in the same fabric as the front and another co-ordinating fabric on the back. For a really striking effect, make the frills from a pretty contrasting colour.

▲ Crowning glory
This pretty frilled duvet cover and pillowcases, which match the curtains and wallpaper, are the crowning glory of this lovely bedroom. The green and ivory colours in the fabric are picked out in the carpet, net curtains and bed valance to complete the effect.

43

Choosing the fabric

Sheeting fabric is 230cm (90in) wide and is usually made from cotton polyester which makes it easy to care for. Its extra width means that both the front and back pieces of a duvet cover can be cut in one piece, so you don't have to worry about pattern matching.

Furnishing fabric is usually 120-130cm (48-50in) wide and is available in a huge range of patterns and colours, with a variety of fibre contents. Choose a washable fabric made of cotton or mixed fibres and pre-wash it to prevent shrinking later.

The furnishing fabric will need to be pieced together on the front and back of double or king-size duvet covers to make up the required width. For professional results, use a full width of fabric in the centre of each piece, with a narrower, matched strip along each side.

Fabric requirements

The amounts given below are for frilled duvet covers made from **sheeting fabric** where the frills have a fullness of one and a half times the length of the seam. For fuller frills, add the depth of one extra frill piece.

(If using **furnishing fabric**, allow two lengths of fabric for both the front and back plus the depth of an extra pattern repeat for each piece to allow for matching. Add the depth of the required number of frill pieces. Since a double duvet with double frill requires 10.3m (11¼yd) furnishing fabric, consider making the back piece or frills from a much cheaper fabric.)

For a **single duvet cover with single frill** you will need 5m (5½yd) of 230cm (90in) sheeting fabric. For a single with **double frill** you will need 5.5cm (6yd) of sheeting fabric. However if the pattern on the fabric does not have a specific direction, you can place the main pieces sideways enabling you to make the cover from less fabric – 4m (3½yd) with a **double frill** and 3.5m (3⅞yd) with a **single frill.**

for a **double duvet cover with single frill** you will need 5m (5½yd) of 230cm (90in) sheeting fabric. For a **double duvet cover with a double frill** you will need 5.5m (6yd).

For each **frilled pillowcase** with single or double frill you will need 1m (1yd) of 230cm (90in) sheeting fabric or 1.7m (1¾yd) of furnishing fabric.

Other materials

Matching sewing thread
Fastening tape – velcro, zip or press fastener type – for the duvet cover
Bias binding and other trimmings are optional

MAKING A DUVET COVER WITH DOUBLE FRILL

1 Cutting out Cut out two pieces of fabric the size of the duvet, adding 10cm (4in) to the length and 3cm (1¼in) to the width. Standard duvet measurements are given on page 40. For a finished frill 12cm (4¾in) wide, cut out fabric strips 27cm (10¾in) wide to make up a piece 1½-2 times the length of the edges to be frilled.

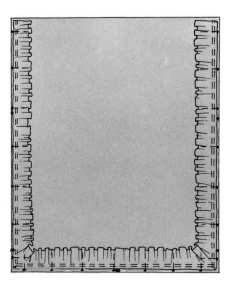

2 Making the frill Join the strips of fabric together with 1.5cm (⅝in) seams. Press seams flat, then fold the frill in half lengthways, right sides together, and stitch seams at the ends. Trim, turn right sides out and press again.

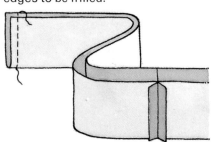

3 Preparing the duvet pieces Turn a double 2.5cm (1in) hem along the bottom short end of each main piece. Pin and machine stitch.

4 Equal parts Divide the frill into six equal lengths, and mark along the long raw edges. Measure the duvet edges to be frilled and divide and mark into 6 equal parts.

5 Gathering the frill Run two rows of gathering threads through both layers of fabric close to the long raw edges of the frill, stopping and starting at the marks.

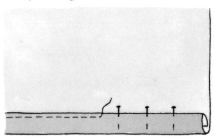

6 Attaching the frill With right sides together and raw edges level, pin the frill to the front, matching the marks. At the top of the front, the finished ends of the frill should be placed level with the seamline. At the bottom of the front, the frill should be placed with the seamline just above the edge of the hem. Pull up the gathers to fit, allowing extra fullness at corners for ease. Snip into corners and tack.

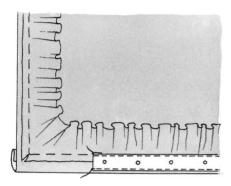

7 Attaching the fastening Along the hemmed edge of each main piece attach the fastening as in steps 2 and 3 for a reversible duvet cover (see page 41). On the piece with the frill, the tape covers the raw edge of the frill.

8 Stitching side seams Pin the two main pieces right sides together and edges matching. Stitch from the bottom edge, over the tape until you are just past the hem. Then stitch near the hem to the side seam, and along the side seam to the top, as shown. Repeat for the other side.

9 Finishing off Tuck the frill away from the top seam and pin to ensure it is not caught in the stitching. Pin and stitch the top seam. Overlock the raw edges together, or trim and zigzag to prevent fraying. Turn the cover out through the opening, spread out the frill and press.

▲ Country charm
The charming appeal of the rustic interior lies in its freshness and simplicity. Here, a subtly patterned, creamy fabric is used for the pillowcases which are frilled for feminine attraction.

MAKING FRILLED PILLOWCASES

1 Cutting out For the front and back of each pillowcase, cut two pieces of fabric 6cm (2½in) longer and wider than the size of the pillow. For the flap cut a piece 20cm (8in) by the width of the pillow plus 6cm (2½in). For a finished double frill 4cm (1½in) wide, cut strips 11cm (4½in) wide to make a total length 1½ times the measurement round the pillow.

2 Preparing the frill Join the frill pieces into one large loop, taking standard, 1.5cm (⅝in) seam allowances. Press seams open, then fold in half lengthways, wrong sides together and press again. Measure the length of the frill, divide and mark into four and run two rows of gathering threads close to the raw edges, stopping and starting at marks.

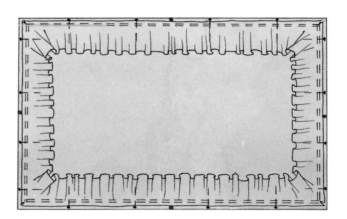

3 Attaching the frill Measure round the front piece and mark in four equal sections. Pull up the gathering threads on the frill and pin to the front, raw edges matching. Snip frill at corners and tack in place.

4 **Hemming** Stitch a double 1.5cm (⅝in) hem along one short edge of the back piece. Stitch a double 1cm (⅜in) hem along the lower edge of the flap.

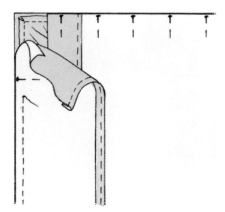

5 **Stitching seams** Put the back and front pieces together, right sides facing, with all edges matching except the hemmed edge of the back which will fall short. Place the flap right side down on top so that the long raw edge lines up with the protruding front edge. Pin, tack and stitch all round taking a 1.5cm (⅝in) seam allowance.

6 **Finishing off** Neaten the raw edges with overlock stitch or by trimming the seams and then stitching together with zigzag stitch. Turn the pillowcase right side out, folding the flap inside, and press.

SINGLE FRILLS

Duvet covers and pillowcases can be made with single frills, with the raw edge finished with a narrow hem or bound with bias binding. A contrast binding can be used to highlight one of the colours in the fabric, or to add zest to a plain fabric.

To make the frill, cut strips of fabric the finished width of the frill plus 1.5cm (⅝in) for seam allowances, and cut the main pieces as above. Join the srips with french seams, attach the binding to one long raw edge or turn a narrow double hem. Continue from step 3 onwards (for duvet cover or pillowcase).

BINDING THE EDGES

1 **Making the binding** Cut strips of fabric on the bias twice as wide as the finished width of the binding plus 1cm (½in). Join strips to make up the required length plus 1.5cm (⅝in). Press the strip in half lengthways. Press the raw edges 5mm (¼in) to the centre. Pressing can be done in one go with a tape maker, or you can use ready-made bias binding which is already folded.

▲ *Attractive ending*
Pillowcases trimmed with frills on the outside ends only, create an attractive and unusual effect.

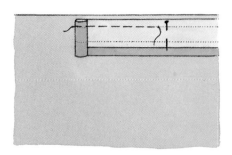

2 **Pin and stitch** Turn in 1.5cm (⅝in) at one end of the binding. Starting at this end, place one long raw edge of the bias binding to the raw edge of the fabric, right sides together. Pin and stitch, following the first fold in the binding.

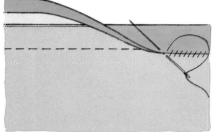

3 **Finishing off** Fold the binding over to the wrong side so that the centre fold in the binding is level with the edge of the fabric. Tuck the other edge of the binding under along the last fold and hand stitch to the fabric to complete.

Edged pillowcases

The Oxford style, or flanged pillow-case is perhaps the most versatile of all the pillowcase styles, and offers a wealth of opportunity for trimming ideas. Since the flange is ungathered, it shows off ribbon, braid and embroidery to good effect, and since it isn't the part you sleep on, it can be embellished with embossed, or raised trimmings without any discomfort.

An Oxford pillowcase is quite straightforward to make, but it does require careful cutting and a certain amount of hand stitching. If you don't have the time or inclination to make one, you could simply buy a ready-made pillowcase and use the trimming ideas given here to transform it into something to be treasured.

▲ Oxford blue
Oxford pillowcases have a simple charm and elegance which is very appealing. Made from crisp blue and white fabrics such as these, they need very little extra adornment to grace the bed with style.

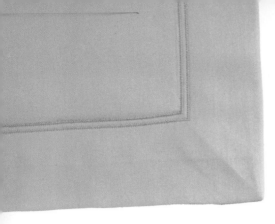

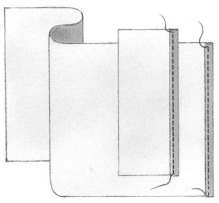

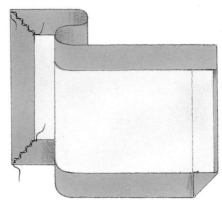

OXFORD PILLOWCASE

1 Cutting out Each 75 × 50cm (29½ × 19¾in) pillowcase requires 80cm (⅞yd) of 230cm (90in) wide sheeting fabric, or 130cm (1½yd) of 120cm (48in) cotton or linen. For the front, cut out a piece of fabric 98cm (38½in) wide and 72cm (28½in) long. For the back, cut a piece 81cm (32in) wide and 52cm (21in) long; and for the flap, cut a piece 20cm (8in) wide and 52cm (21in) long.

2 Stitching the hems On one long edge of the flap, turn 1cm (½in) and then another 1cm (½in) to the wrong side to make a double hem; pin and stitch. Repeat to stitch a double hem along one short edge of the back.

3 Making the flange On the front piece, turn 5mm (¼in) and then 5cm (2in) to the wrong side all the way round. At each corner, fold the fabric under at an angle to make a mitre and trim the excess fabric to reduce bulk; press. Pin the flange, and then carefully slipstitch the mitred corners in place, making sure stitches don't go through to the right side where they will show.

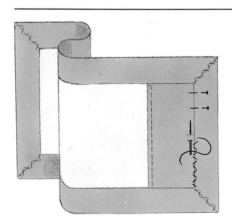

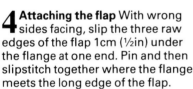

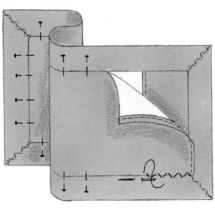

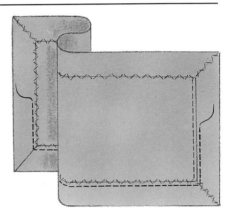

4 Attaching the flap With wrong sides facing, slip the three raw edges of the flap 1cm (½in) under the flange at one end. Pin and then slipstitch together where the flange meets the long edge of the flap.

5 Attaching the back With wrong sides facing, place the back piece on the front so that the hem just overlaps the flange at the flap end. Slip the three raw edges of the back piece under the flange; pin and slipstitch together.

6 Finishing off Working from the back of the pillowcase, machine stitch all round, 3mm (⅛in) from the inside edge of the flange; make sure you don't catch the back opening as you stitch. For added decoration, do this in a close zigzag stitch, using a thread in a toning colour; press to finish.

Simple decorative ideas

Whether you have made an Oxford pillowcase yourself or bought one ready-made, a simple trimming will add that personal touch. A row of braid or machine embroidery, or a shaped edge neatened with zigzag stitch, is all you need to transform the pillowcase. For a really pretty finish, nothing is nicer than a lace and ribbon trim, and for more experienced home sewers, a quilted or scalloped flange will be the crowning glory of the pillowcase.

Braids and piping

Dressmaking trimmings are usually soft enough to trim pillowcases. Ric-rac braid and double piping work particularly well, and will add a flamboyant touch to bed-linen.

Stitch coloured ric-rac near the outer edge of the flange or in the middle. Double piping, or flexible Russian braid can be pinned in a wavy line or in loops and swirls and then stitched in place.

Lace edge Select lace with one scalloped or shaped edge and stitch to the flange on the front of the pillowcase with the shaped edge at the outer edge of the flange. At the corners, fold the lace under in line with the mitre on the flange; stitch and then trim off the excess fabric. Pin satin ribbon over the straight edge of the lace, mitring it at the corners and stitch along both long edges.

Machine embroidery If your sewing machine does embroidery stitches, pick out a favourite pattern and stitch on the front, close to the outer edge of the flange. If you like, stitch further rows towards the middle.

If your machine only does straight or zigzag stitch, sew rows of close zigzag in different colours for a ribboned effect, or stitch wavy lines in running stitch all round.

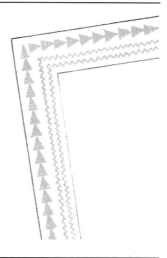

Zigzag edge Shape the edge of the flange by drawing zigzags or scallops with tailor's chalk, and then stitch along the line with a close zigzag stitch. Use a cardboard tube, eggcup or compass to get neat curved lines for the scallops, and for zigzags, use a ruler to measure and mark off even points. Carefully trim the excess fabric close to the stitching. On a plain pillowcase, use the same colour for the stitching round the inner edge of the flange for a really smart finish.

tip

Protective backing
When giving a pillowcase a zigzag edge or doing machine embroidery, tear-away backing will make things easier by providing reinforcement, and preventing stitch distortion. Simply pin the tear-away backing behind the fabric and stitch; then tear off the excess backing when stitching is complete.

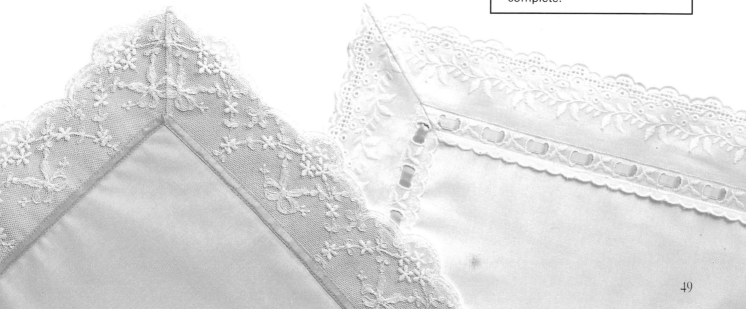

QUILTED FLANGE

For a luxurious and unusual effect, add lightweight wadding to the flange, as you make it, slipping it in place after you have stitched the mitred corners.

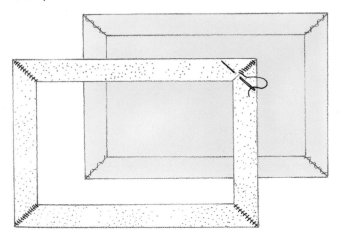

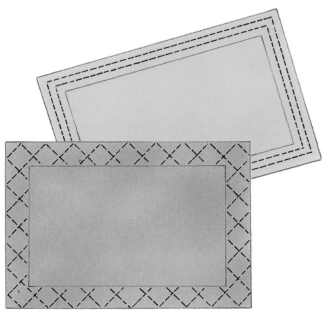

1 Adding wadding Follow steps 1-3 for a flanged pillowcase. Cut strips of wadding 5cm (2in) wide (the width of the finished flange), then place on top of the flange and cut the ends on the diagonal to match the mitres. Butt the two edges together at each corner and stitch together by hand, then slip the frame of wadding into the flange and tuck the 5mm (¼in) turning round it.

2 Quilting the flange Finish making the pillowcase following steps 4-6 for a flanged pillowcase, pinning the flange securely as you sew to hold the wadding in position. Quilt the finished flange in a matching thread, using a quilting bar on the machine for even rows. Stitch in diamond patterns or channels; or if you are more experienced, opt for one of the more complex quilting patterns.

SCALLOPED FLANGE

1 Cutting and stitching Cut out and make up the pillowcase, following steps 1-3 for a flanged pillowcase, but stitching the mitres with very small stitches, and taking particular care not to go through to the front of the pillowcase.

2 Stitching the scallops Carefully turn the flange wrong side out and press. Mark small scallops all the way round the edge, taking care to get a full scallop at each corner, and rounding off the corners if necessary for a good fit. Use a cardboard tube or compass to make even scallops. Pin the flange together, then stitch along the scalloped line taking small stitches.

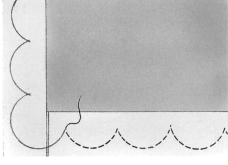

3 Finishing off Trim 1cm (⅜in) beyond the stitching and make snips to, but not through the stitching every 2cm (¾in) for ease. Turn through to the right side and finish making the pillowcase following steps 4-6 for the flanged pillowcase.

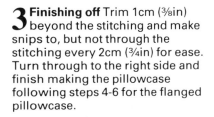

Quilted bedspreads

▲ Quilted comfort
The simplicity of the diamond quilting design on this bedspread is perfectly suited to the main fabric, giving it fullness and a luxuriously padded look, without detracting from the delicate floral pattern as a more elaborate design would.

Quilting gives a bedspread body and shape, as well as providing extra warmth on chilly nights. Even the most basic quilted design, like the simple diamond pattern shown here, will show off your chosen fabric to the full.

When planning a quilt, take the colour and pattern of the fabric into account and choose a quilting pattern and sewing thread accordingly. If the fabric is covered with evenly spaced motifs, emphasize them by centring each one in its own quilted square or diamond. Stripes and checks can be quilted along or in-between their lines, or even at an angle to the main pattern. Plain glazed cottons look stunning quilted with thread in a darker shade, particularly if an intricate design is used, but for all-over patterns keep to a simple quilting design in a toning thread to avoid making the quilt too busy.

Fabrics

Although ready-quilted fabric is available, the choice of fabric and the style of the quilting is limited. Quilting the fabric yourself gives you a far broader choice, allowing you not only to match the bedspread perfectly to other fabrics and colours in the bedroom, but also to experiment with the size and style of the quilted design to achieve different effects.

Firm, closely woven furnishing cottons are best for quilting large items such as bedspreads, as they provide the firm base needed for the stitching. Avoid sheer and loosely woven fabrics, which tend to become distorted when stitched, and through which the wadding underneath is often visible. The choice of fabric colour and pattern is virtually limitless, but do make sure that your chosen fabric is easy to launder, fairly crease-resistant and also reasonably hardwearing.

Joining fabric widths

If making a double, a king-size or even a floor-length single throw-over bedspread, it is unlikely that you will be able to buy fabric wide enough to make these from a single piece; to gain the required width you will need to seam together two or more widths of fabric. Rather than joining these with an unsightly central seam, use a full width of fabric for the centre of the bedspread, with two narrower widths (generally one full width of fabric cut in half lengthways) stitched to each side. Full details on joining fabric widths, and matching the pattern across the seam, are given in *Making a throw-over quilted bedspread*.

Materials

Firm furnishing fabric the chosen size of the bedspread, plus a 1.5cm (⅝in) seam allowance all round (see the section on joining fabric widths)
Lining fabric the same size as the main fabric
Lightweight wadding (batting) the chosen size of the bedspread (see step 7 of *Making a throwover quilted bedspread*)
Covered piping cord (optional) to fit around the edges of the bedspread, plus 10-15cm (4-6in) for ease (see step 1 of *Trimming with piping*)
Sewing thread for quilting
Calculator, squared paper and **pencil** to draw up a small-scale plan of the quilt
Tailor's chalk, long ruler and **set square** to mark the quilting pattern on to the fabric
Tape measure

MAKING A THROWOVER QUILTED BEDSPREAD

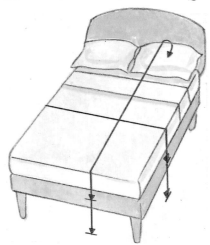

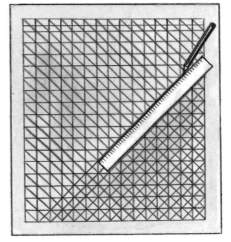

1 Measuring up Always measure up on a made-up bed as the cover will lie over all the bedlinen. First decide how far over the bed edges you want the cover to fall – midway down the side of the bed to reveal a pretty valance, or right to the floor to obscure stored objects or an ugly bed base and legs.

For the width, measure from the chosen depth on one side of the bed over to the same point on the opposite side of the bed. For the length, measure from just behind the pillow at the top of the bed down to the bottom end, taking the tape measure over the edge of the bed to the chosen depth.

Since quilting tends to reduce the overall size of the fabric add 10cm (4in) to both length and width measurements to compensate for this. Also, if you like to tuck the bed cover under the pillows to give a neat appearance, add a further 30cm (12in) to the length measurement.

2 Planning the pattern Decide roughly what size you would like the squares on your quilt to be – as a rough guide, they should be 12-20cm (4¾-8in). To calculate the exact square size needed to fit evenly into your bedspread, divide the width measurement by your desired square size to give the number of squares that will fit the measurement; round up the answer; then divide the measurement by the rounded-up number to give the exact square size.

For example: a bedspread width of 190cm (75in), divided by a square size of 15cm (6in), gives you 12.6 squares, or 13 whole squares when rounded up; divide 190cm (75in) by 13 to give you the exact square size of 14.6cm (5¾in).

As the bedspread is rectangular, you will almost always be left with incomplete squares on the length of the bedspread (if quilting on the diagonal, half-diamonds at the edges are inevitable); plan your bedspread so that incomplete squares lie along the top edge, where they can be hidden behind the pillows. Draw up a plan of the quilt on squared paper.

3 Cutting out If your fabric is wide enough to make the bedspread from a single piece, simply cut out a rectangle to the required size, adding a 1.5cm (⅝in) seam allowance all round. If you need to join two widths of fabric, cut one piece from the main fabric to the required length, plus a 3cm (1¼in) seam allowance at both ends, and a slightly longer piece to allow for pattern matching.

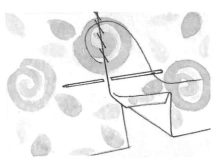

4 Joining widths Cut the longer length of fabric in half lengthways. Take one half-width and fold under 1.5cm (⅝in) to the wrong side along the selvedge; with right sides face up, position the folded edge of the half-width over one selvedge of the main fabric piece, overlapping the two by at least 1.5cm (⅝in) and matching the pattern if necessary. Slip-tack together: bring the needle up through the three layers of fabric on one side of the join, and out at the fold; make tiny stitches across the join through the single layer of fabric and the fold. Trim side pieces to same length as the main piece.

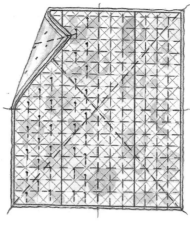

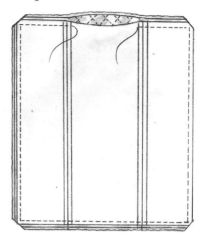

If you are quilting a particularly large bedspread, work the longer diagonals from the centre of the quilt out to the edges. Remove all the tacking stitches.

5 Stitching widths together Turn the side piece over to lie wrong side up, unfold the seam allowance and stitch through the centre of stitches formed along the folded edge. Remove tacking stitches. Attach second half-width to other side of panel. Snip into selvedges and press open. Trim equal amounts from sides to make quilt required width, plus a 1.5cm (⅝in) seam allowance on each side.

6 Marking the pattern Lay the top fabric out flat, with right side up. Use tailor's chalk and a long ruler to mark out the quilting design on the fabric, using your mini-plan as a guide. Begin by marking out the longest diagonals, then mark up all the shorter diagonals, making sure they are perfectly parallel and at an equal distance apart. Use a set square to ensure that all the angles of the diamonds are perfect right angles. If you can use a quilting bar confidently, do not chalk in every line, but only the main diagonals and a few others as reference points.

7 Joining widths of wadding To make up a piece of wadding the same size as the bedspread, you will probably need to join widths together. Line up the wadding pieces, with side edges butting, and stitch together with a wide herringbone stitch.

8 Seaming the wadding Lay the wadding out flat and centre the main fabric over it, right side up. Starting at the centre of the bedspread, pin and tack out to the corners and to the middle of each side edge. Then pin and tack a series of parallel lines 20cm (8in) apart, running across the quilt from one side to the other, and down it from top to bottom; you will find that the wadding spreads out a little as you tack. Finally, pin and tack around the outer edges of the quilt.

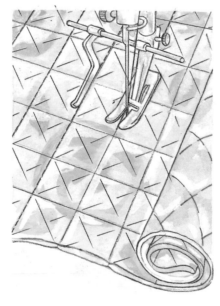

9 Quilting the fabric Experiment on spare pieces of fabric and wadding to find a suitable stitch size – you will need to use a size slightly larger than average. With the fabric face up, begin the quilting by straight-stitching along one of the two longest diagonals, following the chalked line (see machine-quilting tips). Then swing the quilt round and straight-stitch along the other longest diagonal.

Following the chalked pattern and, if you have one, using a quilting bar set to the desired distance, stitch along all the diagonals going in one direction, before swinging the quilt round and stitching along those running in the opposite direction.

10 Attaching the lining Make up the lining to the same size as the bedspread, including a 1.5cm (⅝in) seam allowance all round, joining widths if necessary.

Lay out the quilted fabric, fabric side face up, and place the lining over it, matching the edges and with right sides together. Pin, tack and stitch round the edges, taking a 1.5cm (⅝in) seam allowance and leaving a 45cm (18in) opening in the middle of one edge.

Trim the corners and seams, cutting off the wadding close to the stitching, and turn the bedspread through to the right side. Turn in the opening edges and slip-stitch them together.

tip

Machine-quilting tips
Supporting the fabric When machine-quilting a large item like a bedspread, make sure the bulk of the quilt is supported as you stitch. If it is allowed to hang free over the edge of the table, it will pull during stitching and result in uneven stitch lengths; either work on a very large table or drape the bedspread over a second table or chair.
Working the centre To work the centre of the bedspread, keep the sides rolled up, with the largest section of quilt to the left of the machine foot, and the smaller section tightly rolled to fit under the arm of the sewing machine. If the bedspread is very large, work it from the centre out to the edges, rather than from one side to the other.

TRIMMING WITH PIPING

Trimming the bedspread with fabric-covered piping gives you the opportunity to link it to other fabrics and colours in the bedroom, as well as giving the outline of the quilt added definition and a professional finish.

1 Making the piping Make up the quilt as usual, following steps 1-9. Measure right the way round the outer edge of the quilt to assess how much piping is needed. Follow the instructions for making fabric-covered piping (see page 12) to make-up the required length, plus 10-15cm (4-6in) for ease; use fairly thick piping cord, with a toning or contrast fabric for the bias strips.

2 Attaching the piping Lay out the quilt, with fabric side face up. Pin and tack the covered piping around the edges of the bedspread, with the cord lying innermost and with the stitching line along the piping 1.5cm (⅝in) from the outer edge of the bedspread; to help the piping fabric lie flat, snip into it at the corners, up to the stitching line.

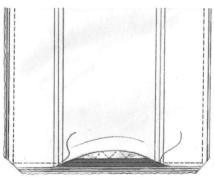

3 Finishing the quilt Make up the lining as usual and place it over the bedspread, matching the edges and with right sides together. Pin, tack and stitch round the bedspread edges through all layers, taking a 1.5cm (⅝in) seam allowance, and leaving a 45cm (18in) opening in the middle of one edge. At the opening, stitch through all layers except the lining. Remove tacking stitches, trim corners and seams, and turn the bedspread through to the right side. Turn in the open edges and slip-stitch the lining to the main fabric.

▼ Topping idea
Added length allows this quilted cover to tuck beneath the pillows.

Pattern quilting

Quilting has always been valued as much for its decorative appeal as for its more practical qualities of warmth and durability. It gives a fabric body and volume, and can also enhance the design if used to outline single motifs or the overall pattern. Emphasize the images on a floral fabric by quilting around flowers and leaves, or stitch around the shapes and splashes of colour in an abstract design to add impact.

Although quilting around motifs is less straightforward than quilting a basic trellis design, it can still easily be done by machine, provided the motifs are not too small and intricate. If your fabric is patterned with large and small motifs, only quilt the former to make up the dominant part of the design. If you wish, the more delicate motifs can be quilted afterwards, either by hand or machine.

With a strong or elaborate pattern, use a thread that blends in with the background; on more subtle designs, accent the motif outlines with a contrasting colour. For items like a bedspread, use a firm, closely woven furnishing cotton, which gives a firm base for the quilting. Make sure that your chosen fabric is easy to clean and reasonably hardwearing.

▼ Freestyle quilting
Stitching around the motifs on a fabric brings its design to life, giving it body and movement. Follow the outlines of each motif, or deviate from them slightly to create complementary patterns.

Materials

Firm furnishing cotton – see steps 1 and 2 for quantity
Lining fabric the same size as the main fabric
Backing fabric for quilting, the same size as the main fabric
Lightweight 2oz wadding the same size as the main fabric
Sewing thread for quilting
Tape measure
Scissors

QUILTED MOTIF BEDSPREAD

1 Measuring up Make sure the bed is fully made up before you begin to measure it. Decide how far over the edge of the bed you would like the cover to fall – midway down the base or right to the floor. For the length, measure from just behind the pillows down to the bottom of the bed, taking the tape measure over to the required depth. For the width, measure from the required depth on one side of the bed over to the same point on the opposite side.

2 Cutting out When you have established the finished size of bedspread, cut out the fabric to the correct size, adding a further 6cm (2½in) all round for seams and shrinkage during quilting; join fabric widths where necessary, making sure you match the pattern across the seams. If you wish to tuck the bedspread under the front of the pillows for a neater appearance, add a further 30cm (12in) to the length. Cut out and make up the lining fabric and the wadding to the same size. (For full details on joining fabric and wadding widths, see pages 52-53.)

▲ *Textured flowers* *The leaf and floral motifs on these bedspreads have been carefully quilted, giving the fabric design a textured, three-dimensional effect.*

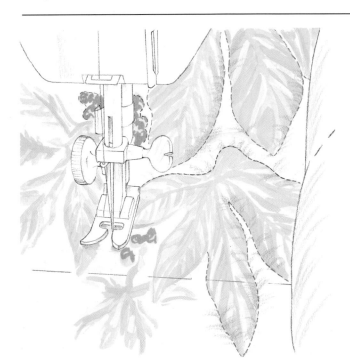

5 Stitching around the motif Carefully stitch around the outline of your chosen motif, trying to maintain a steady rhythm and speed – this will be easier if you plan your stitching sequence in advance. When stitching around sharp curves and points, such as leaf tips, make sure you stitch right to the edge of the motif, and pivot the needle to avoid distorting the fabric.

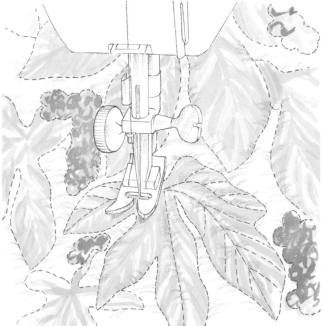

6 Emphasizing the design To add further interest and emphasis to the motifs, quilt in any details that immediately catch your eye, such as the edges of the petals within a rose motif, or the veins on a leaf. As well as adding a touch of realism, this will give the bedspread a wonderfully textured appearance. For natural motifs, like flowers, use a matching thread to fill in detail, so that the eye is drawn to the enhanced design rather than the colour of the thread.

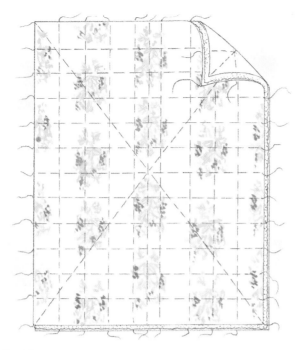

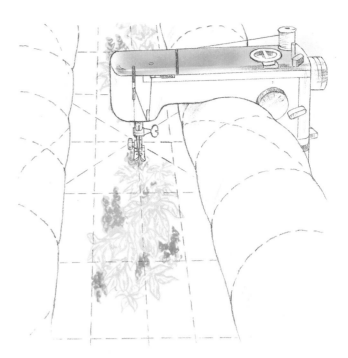

3 **Tacking the wadding to the fabric** Sandwich the wadding between the backing fabric and the main fabric, with the main fabric right side up. Starting at the centre of the bedspread, pin and tack through all layers, working out to each corner, and then to the middle of each side edge. Then pin and tack a series of lines across and down the quilt, spaced about 20cm (8in) apart, to form a grid.

4 **Getting started** Before you begin, practise quilting around motifs on a spare piece of fabric and wadding, until you find the correct stitch length and tension. When you are satisfied, it's best to start with a fairly large motif at the centre of the bedspread. Tightly roll up the sides of the quilt and slip one roll under the arm of the sewing machine – this will make it easier for you to manipulate the quilt while working the centre. If possible work on a large table.

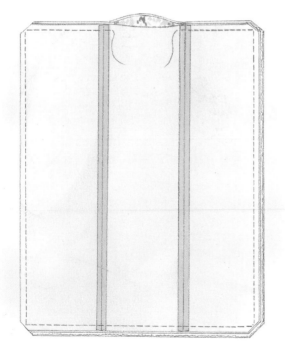

7 **Attaching the lining** Quilt the whole bedspread, working from the centre out to the edges. Then lay out the quilted bedspread with the right side up, and centre the lining over it, with right sides together. Pin and stitch round the edges, taking a 1.5cm (⅝in) seam allowance and leaving a 45cm (18in) opening in the middle of one edge. Trim the corners and seam allowances, then turn through to the right side. Turn in the opening edges and slipstitch together. (For details on piping the bedspread, see page 54.)

▼ *Motif detail The dominant motifs are quilted in a thread whose colour matches the background exactly. The smaller motifs are left unquilted to avoid the design becoming too fussy.*

Quilted appliqué

By combining your quilting skills with basic appliqué, you can create stylish fabric borders for a set of pillowcases. For fully co-ordinated bedlinen, use motifs from leftover bedspread fabric, or from a similar design. Quilting the motifs before you appliqué them to the pillowcases gives them a soft, contoured look, perfectly suited to plump pillows.

Make up a design from a series of motifs scattered down the side of the pillow or, for a more subtle effect, use a single motif in a corner. On a small project like a pillowcase, hand-quilting is always an option, so feel free to choose dainty, intricate motifs. For comfort's sake, always stitch motifs down the side of the pillowcase.

MOTIF PILLOWCASES

1 Cutting out the motifs Plan a rough design and decide which motifs you want to use. Roughly cut out each motif from the main fabric, leaving a 5cm (2in) border all round. For each motif, cut out a piece of wadding and one of backing fabric to the same size.

2 Stitching the motifs Sandwich the wadding between the backing fabric and the wrong side of the motif, and pin and tack together around edges. Straight stitch round the motif, carefully following its outline and stitching through all layers. Stitch in any detail within the motif as well, to add interest and texture. Trim the fabric and wadding to just outside the stitching line.

3 Attaching the motifs Pin each motif separately in position on the pillowcase, arranging the design to achieve the best effect. If the pillowcases are intended to match the bedspread, place the motifs in a similar layout as the original pattern. Use a machine or handworked satin stitch to stitch the motifs in place, working round the outside of each one and covering the raw fabric edges.

Relief effect
To create different areas of relief on a motif, add layers of wadding or cut sections away; for example, give the petals of flowers a fuller effect by cutting wadding away at their base.

▼▶ Sweet dreams
Plain pillowcases are greatly enhanced by the addition of quilted motifs. If short of time, simply stitch a strip of decorative fabric, down the side of the pillowcase to create an equally stylish effect.

Gathered bed valance

A gently gathered valance is an attractive addition to the bed, softening its hard lines and giving it a touch of luxury. It will conceal a bed base which no longer co-ordinates with the room's colour scheme and will cover the gap between the bed base and the floor – ideal if you use the space under the bed for storage.

The valance is made from two main pieces – the base and frill – with the frill attached to the base piece so that it will run along both sides and the foot of the bed. Since only the frill is seen when the valance is in place, the base piece can be made from a cheaper piece of fabric, or even an old sheet. For even more economical results, the frill can be attached to a strip of fabric which tucks under the mattress.

By carefully choosing the fabric for the valance, you can make it into a real feature of the bed. Make it in a plain or patterned fabric, matching the main

▲ Mix and match
Two fabrics used on the bed drapes and pillowcases have been cleverly joined in the valance so that the stripe alternates with the main motif.

colour to the colour of the pillowcases or to one of the colours in the duvet cover. If the duvet cover is piped, then match the main colour in the valance to the piping.

▶ **Old world charm** *A lovely double bed with iron bedsteads has been given a long, very full valance for an old-fashioned effect which is in keeping with the style of the bed.*

Measuring up

For the base piece measure the length and width of the bed base, and add 4.5cm (1¾in) to the length and 3cm (1¼in) to the width for hem and seam allowances. For the frill measure from the top of the bed base to the floor, and add 6.5cm (2⅝in). Cut and join strips this wide to make up a piece one and a half to twice the length of two sides and the foot of the bed.

   Here are the average bed base sizes:
Single 90 x 190cm (3 x 6ft 3in)
Double 140 x 190cm (4ft 6in x 6ft 3in)
Queen-size 150 x 200cm (5ft x 6ft 6in)
King-size 180 x 200cm (6ft x 6ft 6in)
Valance drop 30-35cm (12-14in)

MAKING A GATHERED VALANCE

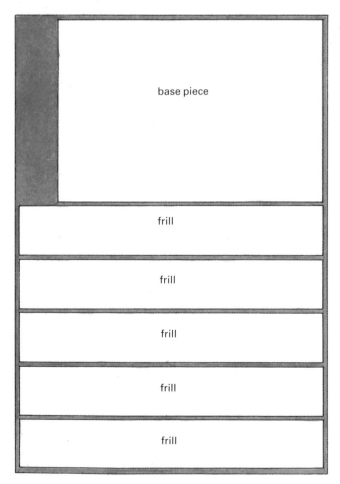

1 Cutting out For a single bed you will need a base piece plus 4 frill pieces cut across the width of the sheeting fabric. For a double, queen or king-size bed you will need a base piece plus 4-5 frill pieces cut across the width of the fabric, depending on the fullness of the frill required.

2 Preparing the base piece At one short end (the end which will go at the head of the bed) turn a double 1.5cm (⅝in) hem. Pin and stitch.

3 Preparing the frill Join the frill pieces together with french seams to make one long strip (see page 85). Pin and stitch a double 1.5cm (⅝in) hem at each end.

4 Sectioning the fabric Measure the length of the frill piece and divide into six to eight equal sections. Measure the sides and lower end of the base piece, and divide the total length into the same number of equal sections. Mark off the sections on the wrong side of the base piece and at the top edge of the frill.

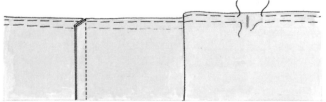

5 Preparing the frill Turn a double 2.5cm (1in) hem along the unmarked edge of the frill. Run two rows of gathering stitches close to the other edge, either side of the 1.5cm (⅝in) seamline. Stop and start the stitching at the chalk marks.

▲ *Patterned valance* Plain white bedding is crisp, clean and fresh looking, but it may sometimes look rather cold. Brighten up the effect by using a patterned fabric for the valance.

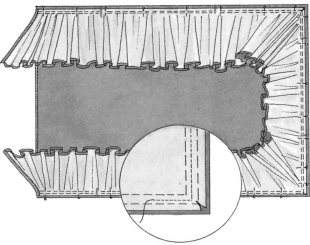

6 Pin and stitch Pin the frill to the base piece at marks so marks match, with right sides facing and raw edges together. Draw up the gathering stitches to fit and arrange gathers evenly, allowing extra fabric at the corners. Snip into seam allowance of frill at corners, then tack and stitch between the rows of gathering stitches. Trim seam allowances and zigzag together.

tip

Neat finish

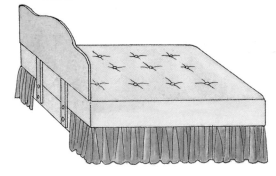

To hide the edge of the frill at the head of the bed, and to give the valance a neater, more tailored appearance, position the frill so that it wraps round to the head end of the base piece by 5cm (2in) on each side. If the bed has a headboard, the frill should stop just at the outside edge of each of the headboard supports.

► *Pretty cover-up*
A bed valance gives an attractive finish to even the most basic bed base. It covers the sides and legs of the base and neatly hides away any items stored underneath.

AN ECONOMICAL VALANCE

A clever and inexpensive way of making a bed valance is to attach the frill to a flap of fabric which is then slipped between the bed base and mattress. The flap is made in three pieces, one for each side and one for the base. The pieces are mitred at the corners to form a three sided frame which sits on the base.

1 Cutting out the frill Cut out strips of fabric for the frill the depth of the frill plus 6.5cm (2⅝in). You will need enough strips to make up a piece one and a half to twice the length of both sides and the foot of the bed.

2 Cutting out the flap Cut out two pieces of fabric for the sides 30cm (12in) wide by the length of the bed plus 4.5cm (1¾in). Cut a third piece for the end 30cm (12in) wide by the width of the bed plus 3cm (1¼in) for seam allowances.

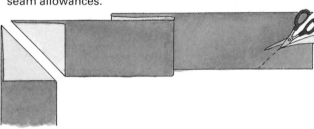

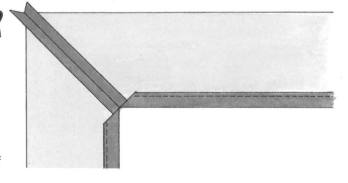

3 Cutting the mitres Take the end piece and fold each short edge over so that it is level with one long edge. Cut along the fold. Fold and cut one short edge of each of the other two pieces so that they will fit at right angles to the end piece.

5 Hemming the flap On the inside edge of the flap, turn under 5mm (¼in), then 1cm (⅜in), allowing the fabric to part naturally at the mitres, and stitch. At the two short ends turn under a double 1.5cm (⅝in) hem; pin and stitch.

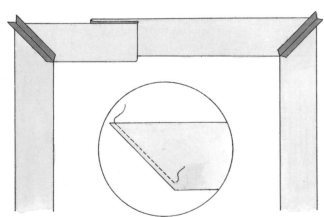

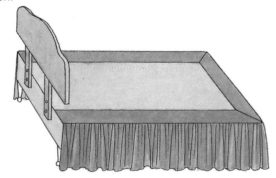

4 Stitching the mitres Place the mitred end of one side piece to a mitre on the end piece, right sides together. Pin and stitch, stopping the stitching 1.5cm (⅝in) from the inner edge.

6 Making up the valance Prepare the frill and stitch to the flap as in steps 4-6 above. Press and then fit on the bed between the base and the mattress.

A simple valanced bedspread

The tailored lines of a fully fitted bedspread can be slightly too formal for some bedrooms, so if you prefer a cosier, softer look, opt for the soft frills of a valanced bedspread.

Different effects can be achieved by varying the fullness of the valance skirt, and also its length. To show off a pretty bed valance and create a double layer of frills, let the skirt hang just below the mattress, or make it floor length to hide an ugly bedstead.

Choose a fabric to complement your bedroom's colour scheme and soft furnishings. To add interest and style, use two different though toning fabrics for the skirt and top panel. This is particularly effective if you use two similar fabrics from the same range, keeping to the same colours but with slightly different patterns. For a summery bedspread, use broderie anglaise for the skirt, and place a pastel pink or blue bed valance behind it.

▲ A perfect choice
Fabrics with a subtle all-over pattern are ideal for valanced bedspreads, and complement their gently fitted lines far more than strong, symmetrical designs. For extra volume and added warmth, quilt the top panel of the bedspread in a simple square or diamond pattern.

Estimating fabric requirements

Details on measuring up the bedspread, together with seam and hem allowances, are given in steps 1 and 2. If making a double or king-size bedspread, you will probably need to join two or more widths of fabric together to make the top panel, as most furnishing fabrics are only available in widths of 120-130cm (48-50in); buy a little extra for pattern matching across the seams.

The valance strips are cut across the width of the fabric and then joined together, so calculate how many strips you need by dividing the width of your valance by the fabric width; allow extra for seam allowances where two strips are joined, and for pattern matching.

Materials

Fabric for bedspread; use a different fabric for the skirt, if preferred
Covered piping the width of the bed and twice its length, plus a little extra for ease, to make up the piping (see page 12).
Saucer or other round object for shaping corners
Matching sewing thread and **tape measure**

SIMPLE BEDSPREAD

1 Measuring up Make up the bed with all the bedlinen, including the pillows. For the finished size of the top panel, measure the length of the bed from just behind the pillows, and its width; add a further 30cm

(12in) to the length if you wish to tuck the bedspread under the front of the pillows for a neater appearance. For the height of the valance skirt, measure from the top of the bed to either just below the mattress or right to the floor, depending on preference. The width of the skirt is twice the bed length, plus its width, multiplied by 1½, 2 or 2½, depending on how full you would like the valance to be.

2 Cutting out For the top panel, cut out a rectangle of fabric to the correct size, adding 4.5cm (1¾in) to the length and 3cm (1¼in) to the width, for seam and top hem allowances; if joining two fabric widths, cut one to the required length, plus 4.5cm (1¾in), and one slightly longer for pattern matching if required. For the skirt, cut out as many strips as are needed to make up the required width; add 4.5cm (1¾in) to the skirt height for a top seam and hem allowance, and 1.5cm (⅝in) to both ends of each strip for seam and side hem allowances. Add extra for pattern matching as necessary.

6 Sectioning the fabric Measure the length of the valance strip and divide it into eight equal sections – this will make gathering the strip easier. Then measure the sides and lower end of the top panel, and again divide the total length into eight equal sections. Use tailor's chalk to mark off the sections around the edges of the panel and along the top edge of the valance skirt, on the wrong side.

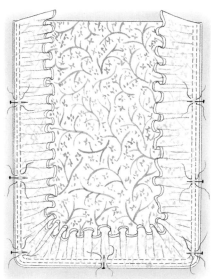

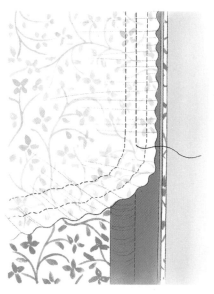

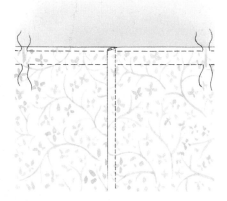

7 Preparing the frill Run two parallel lines of gathering stitches, 2cm (¾in) apart, along the top edge of the skirt, stopping and starting the stitches at each chalk mark. The top thread should lie 6mm (¼in) in from the edge.

8 Pinning and gathering With right sides facing and raw edges together, match up the chalk marks on the top panel and skirt, and pin together over each mark. Working on one section at a time, pull the gathering threads to draw up the skirt fabric to fit the top panel. Check that the folds are evenly spread over each section, and pin in place. Secure the threads by winding them around pins.

9 Stitching together Tack and stitch the valance skirt to the main panel, stitching between the two rows of gathering stitches, 1.5cm (⅝in) in from the edges of the fabric, and close to the piping cord. Snip into the valance seam allowance at the corners for ease. Trim the seam allowances and bind or zigzag together to neaten all the raw edges.

3 **Preparing the top panel** If necessary, join the fabric widths together to make the top panel, making sure you match any pattern across the seams. Using a round object, such as a saucer, as your guide, mark and then trim the two lower corners of the top panel to form a gentle curve – this will give the bedspread a softer finish. (For details on joining widths together, see pages 52-53.)

4 **Adding piping** With the panel right side up and with edges matching, lay the covered piping over the side and bottom edges of the panel, with the stitching on the piping 1.5cm (⅝in) in from the edge. Pin and tack in place, snipping into the piping at the rounded corners for ease. Stitch a double 1.5cm (⅝in) hem along the top edge of the panel, turning under the ends of the piping as you go, for a neat finish.

5 **Joining the valance sections** Join the ends of the skirt sections, enclosing the raw edges with French seams; take 5mm (¼in), then 1cm (⅜in) for the seams, matching any pattern. Pin then stitch a double 1.5cm (⅝in) hem at each end of the strip, and along its bottom edge.

▼ *Keep in trim*
Add a splash of colour to a plain bedspread with a piping trim.

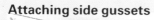
Attaching side gussets

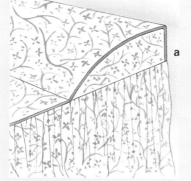

For a perfectly tailored fit over pillows, insert two triangular gussets, one at each side of the bedhead. Make a paper pattern by measuring the height and width of the pillows and drawing these on paper, then joining the two with a soft curve; cut out the pattern and the fabric, adding seam and hem allowances.

Starting at **a**, stitch the straight back edge of the gusset and then the curved edge to the top panel, snipping into the seam allowance to accomodate the curve. Attach skirt to panel as usual.

DAYTIME IDEAS

Pillows can be put in attractive daytime covers and placed on top of the bedspread for a comfy, welcoming look. This will also allow the bedspread to lie perfectly flat for a neat finish at the head of the bed and is a wonderful way to add style to an ordinary bedhead. Make the covers in the same fabric as the bedspread, or in one or more matching fabrics. They can be as simple or extravagant as you wish, so make the most of colourful fabrics and decorative trimmings to enhance a plain or dull bedspread. For extra comfort and variety, cover a few different sized cushions, and scatter these over the bed.

◀ Comfy cushions
A selection of small cushions, covered to match the bedspread, can be scattered over the pillows at the top of the bed, and simply discarded at night. These cushions have been trimmed and decorated with a combination of dainty lace, broderie anglaise and satin ribbon.

▲ Mix and match
A selection of fabrics, shapes and styles has been used to make this charming set of daytime pillow covers, each of which is made from a different patterned fabric, but in the same colours as the bedspread. Large cushions with a matching frill add to the soft, comfy effect.

▼ Plain as can be
Simple, untrimmed daytime covers add softness without being too obtrusive.

Bed coronets

A coronet-style canopy sitting high above the pillows can transform the plainest of beds and give it real designer style. Depending on the choice of fabric and trimmings, and on the fullness of the bed curtains, you can make the coronet as simple or extravagant as you wish, adapting the style to suit the bedroom.

Most coronets consist of a back curtain which sits against the wall behind the bed, and two side curtains which fall in graceful drapes from the front of the coronet. The side curtains are held back at each side of the bedhead by tiebacks or holdback poles, positioned level with the top of the headboard. A semi-circular fabric roof panel is also made to neaten the coronet ceiling, and a valance

pelmet is usually fitted to give the coronet a soft finish.

While it is possible to make your own coronet frame, it is simpler to buy one of the readily available coronet kits currently on the market. These supply you with a pre-shaped semi-circular curtain track, wall brackets and curtain wire to hold the back curtain.

Fabric options

Any fabric that is used in curtain-making is suitable for the coronet. Floral prints will bring a breath of the country into the bedroom, while heavier, darker fabrics in rich colours will give it an opulent, luxurious feel. Experiment with lace, voile and net to achieve a dreamy,

romantic look, ideal in a small bedroom where heavy or busy fabrics can be a touch oppressive.

To add colour and interest to the coronet, use a contrast fabric for the back curtain and to line the side curtains, as suggested in the instructions given. Choose a fabric to suit the colour scheme and other furnishings in the bedroom, or use a decorative trimming or tiebacks to make the link.

▼ *Shades of blue*
By carefully choosing fabric which blends with other colours and furnishings in the bedroom, you can create a coronet that looks stunning, but does not dominate the setting.

Fabric requirements

The amount of fabric used depends on the height of the coronet and the bed size. These instructions use two 120cm (47¼in) fabric widths for the back curtain and one 120cm (47¼in) width of main and contrast fabric for each curtain. For a fuller effect, use 2½ widths for the back curtain and 1½-2 widths for the sides, ensuring the coronet track is long enough to hold them.

Materials

Coronet track set which should include wall brackets, a curved track for the side curtains, a curtain wire for the back curtain, curtain and valance hooks, holding hooks for tiebacks and fixing screws, a pattern for cutting the roof panel and Velcro Hook and Loop to fix it in place

Fabric for the side curtains and valance (see steps for quantities)

Contrast lining fabric for the back curtain and ceiling panel, and to line the side curtains and valance (see steps for quantities)

Heading tape 2.5cm (1in) wide for the side curtains, and 7.5cm (3in) wide for the valance; you will need 2.5m (3yds) of each

Matching threads

▲ **Crowning glory**
A fabric-covered bedhead to match the coronet is a wonderful way to link the bed to your canopy.

MAKING THE CORONET

The cutting out instructions given here are based on the standard furnishing fabric width of 120cm (47¼in). If your chosen fabric is narrower, cut out and join extra widths where necessary.

1 Fixing the track and tieback hooks Decide on the position of the coronet above the bed – the standard height is 213cm (7ft), but take into account the proportions of your bedroom which may dictate a different height. Assemble and fix the track to the wall above the centre of the bedhead, following the manufacturer's instructions. Position and fix the two tieback hooks level with the top of the headboard, one on each side of the bed.

2 Cutting out the back curtain Measure from the curtain wire to the floor, and add 13.5cm (5¼in) for hems and the top casing; cut out two widths of your contrast lining fabric to this length, allowing extra for pattern matching if necessary.

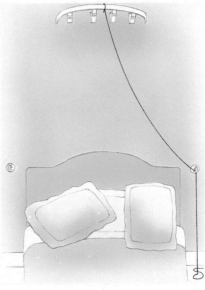

3 Cutting out the side curtains Use a length of string to measure the drop of the side curtains: measure from the curtain track down the side of the bed to the floor, allowing the string to form a gentle drape over the holding hook. Add 3.5cm (1⅜in) to this length for hems and headings. For each side curtain, cut out one width of your main fabric to this length, and one of your contrast lining fabric; allow extra for pattern matching.

4 Making up the back curtain Join the two fabric widths together, with two side seams rather than a central one, and make sure you match the pattern across the seams where necessary (see pages 52-53). Neaten the raw edges and press open. Pin and stitch a double 1.5cm (⅝in) hem down each side edge of the curtains.

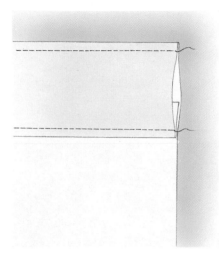

5 Adding a top casing To form the top casing, turn down 1cm (⅜in) and then a further 2.5cm (1in) to the wrong side, along the top edge of the back curtain. Pin and stitch along the hemline, and also along the top folded edge. Pin and stitch a double 5cm (2in) hem along the bottom edge of the curtain. Thread the curtain wire through the casing and hang the curtain right up against the wall.

6 Stitching the roof panel Using the pattern supplied with the kit, cut out two pieces of the contrast fabric. Place the pieces right sides together and pin then stitch all round, leaving a small opening for turning through. Trim the seams and snip into them around the curve. Then turn right side out, fold in the fabric edges of the opening and slip stitch to close.

7 Fixing the panel in place Cut the supplied Velcro strips to the correct length. Stick one side of the Velcro to the track brackets. Pin the other side in position on the fabric roof, then stitch in place. Fix the roof panel in place by pressing the Velcro strips together.

8 Making up the side curtains With right sides together and taking a 1.5cm (⅝in) seam allowance, pin and stitch one length of contrast lining fabric to one length of main fabric down both sides and along lower edge. Snip into seam allowances at the corners and turn right side out. Press the seam to the edge, so no contrast fabric will show on right side. Repeat for second curtain.

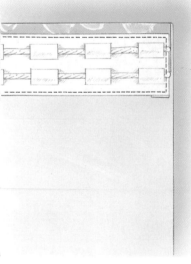

9 Adding the heading tape Treat the two fabrics as one at the top edge. Turn down 2cm (¾in) of top edge to the lining side. Pin the 2.5cm (1in) heading tape over the raw edges, 3mm down from the folded top edge. Knot the tape cords at the front edge and turn under, so that the tape edge is in line with the front edge of the curtain. At the back edge of the curtain, unpick the tape cords and turn under the raw end of the tape in line with the curtain edge. Stitch in place. Repeat on second curtain. Pull up each curtain to required length and hang on track.

10 Cutting out the valance Once the curtains are in place, decide how long you would like the valance to be – generally 30-50cm (11¾-19¾in). Cut two widths of both your main and contrast fabric to this length, plus 3.5cm (1⅜in) for hems and headings, allowing extra for pattern matching if necessary.

11 Stitching the valance Pin and stitch the two main fabric widths together, and the contrast fabric widths, matching the pattern across the seam where necessary. With right sides facing and taking a 1.5cm (⅝in) seam allowance, pin and stitch the main fabric to the contrast fabric down the sides and along the bottom edge. Turn through to the right side and attach the 7.5cm (3in) heading tape exactly as for the two side curtains. Pull up the valance heading tape and hang on to the hooks at the front of the track.

ANOTHER HEADING

Rather than making a valance for your coronet, stitch an attractive stand-up frill along the top edges of the side curtains, as shown in the opening picture. This looks particularly effective if the same heading technique is used on other curtains in the room.

Simply allow an extra 20cm (8in) on the curtain length for turning back above the heading tape, then stitch and gather up the tape as usual. To conceal the join of the curtains at the front of the coronet, attach a fabric rosette where they meet, and complete with matching tiebacks.

tip

Frilled finish
To add style and fullness to a plain coronet, trim the two side curtains and the bottom of the valance with a decorative frill in the same or a co-ordinating fabric.

DECORATIVE TIEBACKS

Imaginative tiebacks or holdback poles provide the finishing touch for a coronet, and greatly enhance the overall impression given by the drape. Position them carefully on a level with the top of the bedhead, and arrange the curtains to fall in a gentle drape at each side of the bed.

▶ **Pretty bows**
If you choose to use metal holdback poles, but want to keep the effect soft and feminine, disguise their metal ends with a full fabric bow. The bows are easily made up in the same fabric as the side curtains, and can then be simply glued to the ends of the holdback poles. To add the final touch, cover the poles with the contrast curtain fabric so they blend into the background.

▲ **Tailored tiebacks** *For a classic finish to your coronet, make a pair of elegant tailored tiebacks in the same fabric as your curtains or contrast lining. Alternatively, opt for one of the more unusual tieback designs, such as a plaited, ruched or bow tieback, or use heavy tassel-trimmed cords for a more luxurious effect. Details on making tiebacks are given on pages 99-106.*

▲ **Ornate rosettes** *Fashionable rosettes will add grandeur to a stately coronet, and can be used as a clever cover-up for metal holdback poles (as here), or to add style to plain tiebacks. Make two-colour rosettes in a combination of your main fabric and contrast lining for a perfectly co-ordinated look, or introduce a new colour to add interest where the coronet fabrics are plain. A third rosette placed centrally over the valance makes a majestic finishing touch.*

Lace panels

Until very recently sheer curtains were chiefly about privacy. They veiled a household from the prying eyes of passers-by, while allowing a diffused light to filter in through the window. To these traditional virtues, another security value can be added: the would-be burglar will find it difficult to survey the scene with screened windows.

Today, sheer curtains can be enjoyed for the range of interior light effects they provide. With an unparalleled choice of easy-care translucent fabrics on the market – from the most intricate laces to the lightest voiles – the choice is about sheer beauty as much as sheer practicality. You can use the fabrics' qualities of texture and drape for dramatic effects, to disguise an ugly window or glorify a pretty one.

Lace panels, like all sheers, tame the light and offer privacy and intimacy.

Unlike plain sheers such as voile and muslin, lace panels look their best hanging straight so that the pattern shows to best effect. However, by using metres of cheaper lace with a heading tape, you can create a window dressing that provides both atmosphere and privacy.

▼ *Graceful lace* *Swathes of lace over and around the window and furniture impart serenity and lightness.*

The range of panels

Now there are many cotton and synthetic mix laces available which offer the patterned charm and texture of antique lace, while being easier to care for. Again, with the country look in mind, it's best to stick to the traditional bridal colours of lace – white or cream.

Lace fabric with distinctive patterns can be bought as separate panels or by the metre. Sold as complete ready-made window coverings, these panels come in a range of set sizes and have the addition of integral eyelets or a casing along the top edge ready for slotting on to fine rods for instant window dressing.

If you prefer to make your own panels, or you have awkward shaped windows, lace can be bought by the metre in a range of different widths. Some narrow widths have integral eyelets or a casing running along one of the selvedge edges, the other edge decorated with a scallop. So buy the metre length to fit the width of your window. This is particularly suitable if you want to cover the lower half of the window, for example, in the kitchen or bathroom. For taller windows, buy the metre length to fit the length of the window and make your own choice of heading and hem.

Lace fabrics are also available with detachable edgings. These borders can be removed and added to hem and top edges to complete the decorative frame round a window covering.

Hanging panels

The quickest and easiest way to hang ready-made and homemade lace panels at a window is to use elasticated wire, a fine brass or wooden pole or one of the new fine plastic rods slotted through a casing at the top of the panel. This is particularly suitable for lightweight lace panels which are not to be drawn back and forth, but used as a permanent screen at the window.

If your homemade panel needs a hem or a casing, make sure that you turn under a double width allowance, which will hide the raw edge of the fabric.

Measure your window area and decide on the style first. Fix your rod or wire in place and plan what width of curtain panel you need. Do you want a fuller look or the lace flat across the window?

If your window is narrower than the fabric width, a cased heading will gather the lace gently on the fitment. In this case, choose an all-over pattern rather than a large motif design.

If you are covering large picture windows, lace panels can be either hung loosely side by side or stitched together.

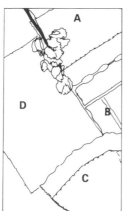

Different lace panels

A – Lace panel with a detachable border. The border simply peels away and can be used as a decorative edge on the hems.
B – Lace panel with an integral border. This can be used sideways across the window with the scallop at the top and base or lengthways.
C – Lace panel with eyelet holes. The lace is slotted over a slimline rod.
D – All-over lace patterns. This fabric is available by the metre in wide measures like furnishing fabrics. All the edges need to be finished.

TO MAKE A CASED HEADING

Decide where the rod or fitment is to be hung and then measure the depth of the window from the sill to the top of the rod. Measure the circumference of the rod, add between 1-3cm ($^3/_8$-$1^1/_4$in) for ease and double this measurement for the casing. This will be the cut length of the panel. Casings for elasticated wires need only be 3cm ($1^1/_4$in) deep.

1 As the hem edge of lace panels is usually decorative, measure the length up from the hem edge. Cut off the excess fabric from the top edge.

2 Turn under the casing allowance twice. Pin and topstitch across the casing close to the folded hem edge. Topstitch across the casing again against the top folded edge.

3 Slot the rod or wire through the casing and hang the lace panel in place.

TO MAKE A STAND HEADING

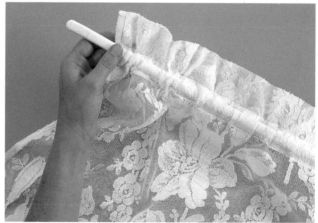

If you allow extra fabric above the casing this will form a short stand or, if the fabric is wider than the window, a slightly gathered frill. Add twice the stand depth to the casing measurement.

Form and stitch the casing along the panel, with the extra fabric between the top line of the casing stitching and the panel head.

◀ *Lace and wood* Here *lace has been used for a simple effect. The lace panel complements both the shape and the handsome wood of the window surround.*

COVERING A WIDE PICTURE WINDOW

To cover a wide window, lace panels can be placed side by side, with edges butting together. In this way the decorative side edges can be left free and visible.

With this method the casing is not made from the lace panels. You will need a length of sheer fabric in the same colour to form a casing. This should be as long as the panel widths and twice the width of the casing depth, plus seam allowances.

Stitching borders
If you prefer to join decorative panels together, instead of butting the edges together, overlay the two edges and machine zigzag stitch together with a wide stitch, following the line of the decorative edge.

1 Lay the lace panels, with edges butting, right side up. Measure up for the length of the finished panels and mark the position of the casing.

2 Fold the sheer fabric strip in half lengthways and pin the raw edges along the marked casing line on the right side of the lace. Stitch in place across the top edges of all the panels. Trim excess lace.

3 Turn the strip to the wrong side, with the seam to the top edge. Pin and zigzag stitch across the folded edge forming the casing. Stitch again close to top edge.

4 When placing two panels side by side, make sure that the design matches across the join.

Looking after lace

Treat lace fabrics in the same way as you would other home furnishings by laundering according to fibre content. Most heavy lace fabrics are cotton or cotton based and substantial enough to withstand a delicate cycle wash in a machine. For preference, and to retain a bright white colour, use a biological detergent. If you are unsure, you can wash these fabrics by hand with a handwashing soap powder.

Allow the lace to dry naturally in an airy place away from direct sunlight.

Synthetic lace fabrics can be washed in the same way, but check their fibre content to choose the correct washing programme. If they become a bit dull and lifeless use a proprietary nylon whitener. If you prefer a warm natural shade for your cotton lace, dip it in cold tea. The longer the curtain is submerged the darker the shade of beige.

▶ *Pretty as a picture* A pair of lace panels are tied back loosely enough to provide a generous sweep and to display the large floral motif. Used like this, lace curtains impart an immediate charm to the window, from without as well as from within. In spite of its delicate appearance, lace is relatively easy to keep fresh and clean.

Sheer curtains

The simplest effect with nets and sheer curtains is a plain, translucent drop of white or off-white fabric. These curtains are usually hung from a lightweight track, pole or rod, using a heading tape or system specially designed for such lightweight fabrics.

Sheers are produced in every size and style, as well as an ever-increasing range of colours. Muslin, lawn, voile, cheesecloth, flax and cotton mixes are all part of the rich sheer picture. Many manufacturers produce their sheer fabrics by the metre in the same standard widths as ordinary curtain fabric, with wider widths for extra large windows. Like lace panels, sheer fabrics can be bought with a casing along one edge and a scalloped or hemmed finish along the opposite edge.

▲ **Spotted charm** White spotted voile hung from a simple curtain track screens this small window. The curtains are swept back and held with ribbon-trimmed rosettes. For night time privacy this kind of curtain can be teamed with an opaque roller blind.

Fabric and effect

The diversity of the sheer fabrics available is equalled by the diversity of effects that can be achieved. By availing yourself of the special qualities of individual fabrics, you can achieve the most distinctive results.

Having selected the fabric, there are innumerable ways of treating it: jardinière styles where the central part of the curtain swoops up in the middle; café curtains that shield the lower part of the window; tiered effects where you can build up layers of curtain all on the same track system; or you can simply drape the fabric without doing any sewing at all. These different styles will be covered in later chapters.

Curtain fittings

Achieving the right sheer effect is not only a question of choosing fabric. The other major consideration is how that fabric is to be hung. Curtains with cased headings stay in position and either hang straight or tie back. If you want to draw the whole curtain back you will need a heading tape with hooks and rings. For example, an elegant white painted pole with curtain rings would be appropriate in a cool, quiet living room or bedroom. A brass rod might be better in the kitchen with its array of pots and pans, and a plastic track in the bathroom.

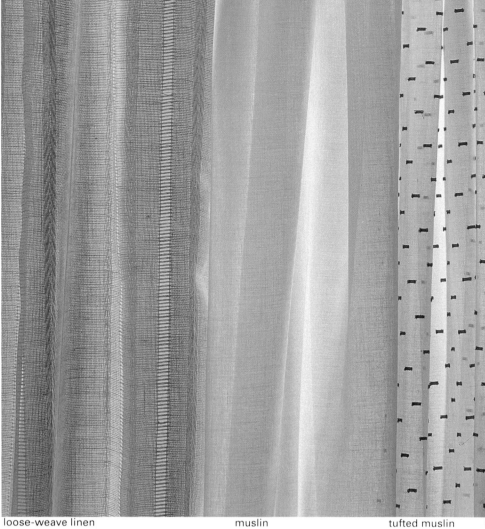

loose-weave linen   muslin   tufted muslin

Covered wire

The simplest way to hang light net curtains is from a length of wire. The white plastic-covered wire is usually sold in packs in different lengths. Also included in each pack are two eyelet screws and two hooks. The eyelets screw into each end of the wire and the hooks into the window frame or surround. Their main drawback is length – a long length of covered wire can sag badly in the centre. To avoid this, cut the wire slightly shorter than the length required so that it is well stretched in position. The curtain is made up with a cased heading and the wire is slotted through and slipped over the hooks at either side of the window.

Some heading tapes incorporate loops along the tape to carry covered wire. With this method you can have the benefit of pleating with the simplicity of a wire hanging.

Telescopic rods

Slimline plastic and metal rods fit inside the window frame. Each rod has an internal spring which tensions the rod to hold it firmly in place. The curtain is finished with a cased heading used to thread it on to the rod before it is tensioned into position. If the curtain has a finished

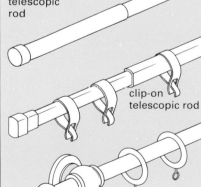

covered wire

telescopic rod

clip-on telescopic rod

wooden pole

top edge, you can choose a rod that can be matched with clip-on rings. These hold the curtain top and slot on to a rod rather like a shower curtain.

Wooden or metal poles

For an emphatic country statement, fit wooden or brass-like poles. They come in a variety of wood shades, painted or stained, and in several metal finishes. Each pole can be purchased in a range of lengths complete with end finials, rings and supporting brackets. The curtain can be attached by rings combined with heading tape or with the pole through a deep casing, or simply throw the fabric over the fixed pole for a stylish effect.

Flexible tracks

Held on simple, easy-to-fit brackets, these white plastic tracks can be bent around curves, making them useful for bays and bow windows. The packs come with brackets and joints which secure the easily bent tracks at the bends of the bays. The curtains are finished with cased headings and slotted on to the track.

Curved steel rods

Available in single or double versions (the double rod allows you to hang cross-

spotted voile   sprigged polyester   printed voile

over nets and valances), these straight rods have curved ends that are held on either side of the window. The central span can be adjusted to length. The curved ends keep the curtain away from the window pane. This type of rod works well with a cased headed curtain.

Traditional curtain tracks

If you are hanging sheer curtains with a heading tape, choose a neat, slim track. Generally, these tracks can be wall or ceiling mounted – held in or outside the window reveal. The tracks can be bought in different lengths but are easy to cut down to size. Pliable enough to bend around bay windows, some tracks are also equipped to hold an additional valance track on the front.

Heading tapes

Sheer fabrics, because of their fineness, give you the opportunity to use some of the more decorative tapes. With the standard heading tapes, the curtains can be gently gathered with a barely visible lightweight tape or, if you prefer, into more elegant pencil pleats. With this type, there is a choice of depth from a neat mini pleat to a deep 10cm (4in) pleat.

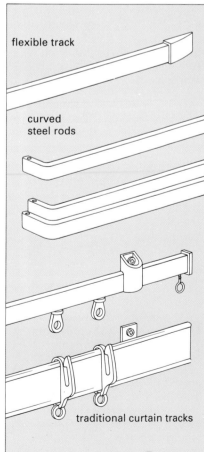

flexible track

curved
steel rods

traditional curtain tracks

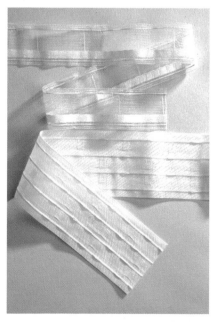

▲ **Heading tapes** *The translucent tape (top) forms a pencil pleat heading. The tape has pockets for curtain hooks and loops for curtain wire giving alternative methods for hanging. The wider tape (below) pulls up to give an attractive smocked heading which looks particularly effective when used with sheers.*

ESTIMATING FABRIC AMOUNTS

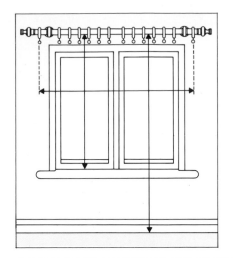

Fix the track Decide on your fitting and fix in place at the window, following the manufacturer's instructions. Covered wire and tension rods need to be positioned inside the window recess, while poles and tracks can be fitted outside.

 If fitted inside the recess, check the depth of the curtain stand above the heading before fitting in place. Outside the window you have a free hand in positioning the fitment, but bear in mind the overall look.

Measure the track length
Depending on the heading tape, multiply by 1½ to 3 times the track length – check with the shop when you buy the tape. Divide this figure by the width of the fabric to find the number of fabric widths or drops needed for each curtain. If the figure falls between two widths, round up to the next full width.

 Measure from the track to the desired length – to the sill or floor. Add the width of the heading tape and twice the hem depth.

To get the total amount of fabric
Multiply this figure by the number of fabric widths. Ask the shop to allow extra fabric to match patterns.

MAKING THE CURTAINS

1 Cutting the widths Make up each curtain in the same way. Straighten the fabric edge, then cut out as many widths of fabric as you need to cover the track, using the chosen heading tape. If there is a distinctive pattern or weave, this should be matched at each join.

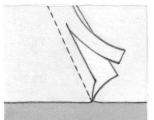 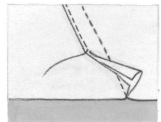 

2 Joining widths If necessary, stitch the fabric widths together into one piece with flat fell seams. Place the two fabric widths with right sides together; pin and stitch 1.5cm (⅝in) from raw edges. Trim one seam allowance down to 6mm (¼in). Fold the wider seam allowance round the narrower allowance and flat against the fabric; press. Pin and stitch down the complete seam along the folded edge.

3 The double hem Turn in both side edges for 2cm (¾in); turn under again for 2cm (¾in) forming a double hem; press and tack. Turn up the lower hem edge in the same way to form a double 5cm (2in) deep hem; press. Check that the base corners look neat.

4 Finishing the hems Stitch the hems in place, by hand or machine, working round the curtain. Remove tacking.

7 The heading tape Stitch heading tape in place, stitching over the cords at the inner edge, but leaving them free at the outside edge.

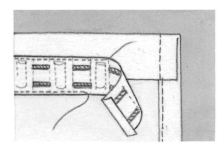 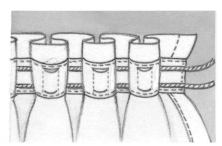 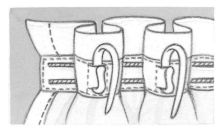

5 Positioning the heading tape Turn down the top edge for the width of the tape, plus the depth of the stand heading. Position the heading tape to the wrong side of the fabric, with base edge just covering the raw fabric edge; pin.

6 The cords At the inside edge of curtain, pull tape cords out from the tape and knot. Turn under tape end in line with curtain edge and trim to 1.5cm (⅝in); pin. At the outside edge, pull the cords out from the right side of the tape. Turn under the end in the same way as before; pin. Tack tape in place, hang on the track and check length.

8 Hanging the curtains Pull up the cords to fit window, then ease gathers evenly across the width. Tie the cords. Hang the curtain on the track with hooks provided, spacing them at about 20cm (8in) intervals.

Austrian blinds

Whether teamed with curtains or used on their own, elegant Austrian blinds are at home in many different types of surroundings, from the simplest country cottage to the grandest town house. Their soft folds and swooping scallops provide the luxurious fullness of curtains, but take up far less room, making them an ideal choice where space around the window is limited.

Like curtains, Austrian blinds are gathered across their width, giving them a full effect whether lowered or raised.

The scalloped effect across the bottom of the blind is created when the blind is pulled up, by means of cords threaded through vertical rows of ringed tape, attached to the blind at regular intervals. Always make the blind a bit longer than the window to retain the scallops even when the blind is lowered.

The choice of fabric will determine the effect created by the blind, whether grand and sophisticated or pretty and informal. Rich fabrics like moiré, slubbed satin or heavy silks will form deep, well-defined folds, and look

▲ Perfect combination
Striped or plain fabrics work well with Austrian blinds, giving a stylish simplicity to their exuberant folds and flounces.

elegant and luxurious, particularly if trimmed with braid or fringing. Crisp cotton chintz bunches up into casual, puffy folds for a fresh, cosy look, and looks smart trimmed with a frill.

If covering a wide window, use two Austrian blinds side by side, rather than a single one, which would sag.

Materials

Note: Austrian blind kits can be bought from most department stores and include most items listed below, except fabric and basic sewing equipment.

Austrian blind track available from department stores

Fabric for the blind and frill trimmings (for quantities, see *Calculating fabric quantities* and step 1 of *Lined Austrian blind*)

Lining fabric

Bias binding 1.5cm (⅝in) wide, in a contrasting shade, to trim the frill

Fabric-covered piping to match binding

Pencil-pleat heading tape to fit across the top of the blind; you will need a length 2½ times the length of the track

Austrian blind tape the length of the blind by the number of tapes required

Non-stretch cord to draw up the blind

Cleat

Matching sewing threads

Tape measure and **tailor's chalk**

Calculating fabric quantities

To ensure accuracy when measuring up for the blind, fix the blind track in place above the window before you begin, and take your measurements from it. If the blind is to lie inside a window recess, fix the track to the recess ceiling. Where it will lie outside the reveal, fix the track 5-10cm (2-4in) above the window, and extend it by this amount on each side to give full coverage of the window.

To calculate the blind's width, multiply the track length by 2½ – this will give you a wonderfully full blind once gathered up by the pencil pleat heading tape. Divide this figure by the width of your fabric to determine how many fabric widths you will need; round up if necessary. An additional width can be split between a pair of blinds for extra fullness.

To calculate the drop, measure from the track down to the windowsill, and add 45cm (18in) for turnings and to ensure that the bottom edge of the blind remains prettily swagged, even when lowered to fully cover the window. To calculate the total amount of fabric needed, simply multiply the drop of the blind by the number of fabric widths. Remember to add on a little extra for pattern matching across the seams. (The fabric quantities needed for making a frill trimming extending down both sides and across the lower edge are given in step 1 of *Lined Austrian blind*.)

LINED AUSTRIAN BLIND

These instructions are for a lined Austrian blind, trimmed with contrast piping and a bound frill. Lining the blind gives it fullness and creates more luxurious swags, as well as making it more durable and giving a neater appearance when viewed from outside.

1 Cutting out Cut out the main fabric to the correct size (see *Calculating fabric quantities*), adding a 1.5cm (⅝in) seam allowance all round; join fabric widths where necessary, being sure to match the pattern across the seams. Cut out the lining to the same size as the main fabric, but deduct 2cm (¾in) from the length. For the double-sided frill, join widths of the main fabric to make up a strip, 17cm (6¾in) deep, and twice the length of the blind plus its width, multiplied by 1½-2.

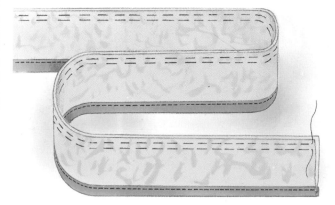

2 Making the bound frill Fold the fabric strip in half lengthways with wrong sides together, and bind the folded edge with the contrast binding. Run two rows of gathering threads along the other long edge, 5mm (¼in) and 1.5cm (⅝in) in from the edge. Draw up the frill to fit round the two sides and lower edge of the blind.

---

tip

Invisible rings

Rather than using Austrian blind tapes, which can sometimes show through the blind and which require lines of stitching down the front, you can thread the pulling cords through rows of clear curtain rings stitched to the back of the blind.

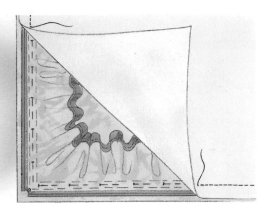

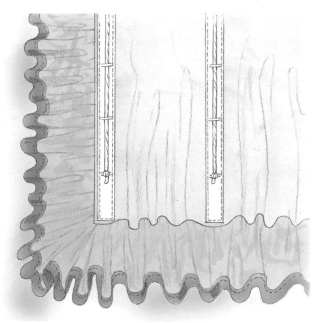

3 Attaching the lining Lay out the main fabric, right side up. Pin and tack the piping and then the frill along the blind's sides and lower edge, with their raw edges lying slightly inside the blind's edges. With side and lower edges matching and right side down, put lining on top. Taking a 1.5cm (⅝in) seam allowance, stitch through all layers down sides and along lower edge. Snip into corners and turn through to right side. Press to lie flat, then tack across top edge.

4 Marking the positions of the tapes Decide how many scallops you would like the blind to have: the vertical Austrian blind tapes are usually placed about 60-75cm (23-30in) apart, to give scallops of 24-30cm (9-12in) on the finished blind, once it has been gathered across its width. Choose a scallop size which divides evenly into the width of your blind. Use tailor's chalk to mark the positions of the tapes on the lining side of blind; the first and last tapes run down the blind's side edges.

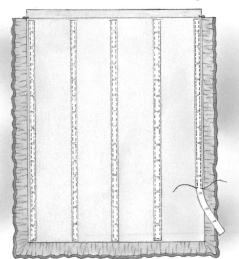

5 Attaching the vertical tapes Cut lengths of Austrian blind tape, the same length as the blind's lining plus 1cm (⅜in); when cutting the tapes, make sure that the bottom loop on each length lies 6cm (2¼in) from the end of the tape, so that the blind will pull up evenly across its width once the cords have been threaded and tied in place. Turn 1cm (⅜in) to the wrong side at the bottom of each tape, then pin, tack and stitch the tapes in position on the blind.

6 Attaching the heading tape Cut a length of pencil-pleat heading tape the width of the blind, plus a little extra for neatening the ends. At the top of the blind, fold the overlapping 2cm (¾in) of main fabric over the lining to enclose its raw edge. Place the pencil-pleat heading tape across the top of the blind on the lining side, enclosing the raw edges of the fabric and vertical tapes; stitch the heading tape in place. Draw up the heading tape to fit the window.

7 Threading the cords For each vertical tape, cut lengths of cord the finished width of the blind plus twice its length. Lay the blind out flat on the floor, with lining side up. Starting at the bottom left-hand corner of the blind, tie the end of one length of cord to the bottom loop on the vertical tape. Thread the cord up through all the loops on the tape. Repeat on all the other vertical tapes.

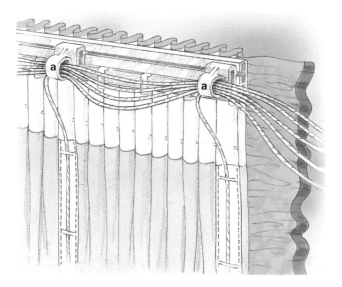

8 Mounting the blind Remove the track from its wall brackets and hook the blind on to the track, as for a curtain. Adjust the position of the track eyelets (**a**) so that there is one above each vertical blind tape. Thread the cords from each vertical tape through the eyelet above, and then through the other eyelets along the track, until all the cords are at one side of the window. The blind track is then replaced on its brackets. Fix the cleat to the wall or window frame next to the blind, about halfway down the window.

9 Checking the blind Pull the cords to check that the blind can be raised and lowered evenly, and adjust the cords where necessary. Once satisfied, lower the blind and double check that all the cords are straight, before tying them together in a knot at the end of the track. Plait the cords together to make a single pulley cord, and trim the ends with scissors to neaten. Pull the blind up to the desired position and secure the cords around the cleat at the side of the window.

Stylish variation

With a few minor alterations in the vertical cording and the addition of imaginative trimmings, Austrian blinds can be given a number of different looks. One popular variation is to shape the blind into a swag and tail arrangement, by simply omitting the vertical tapes at the side edges; this allows the sides of the blind to hang freely, while the centre is gathered up into sweeping swags. The arrangement makes a stunning crown for a window, and looks striking used alone or teamed with a sheer curtain for daytime privacy.

Alternatively, by drawing up the pull cords to different lengths, you can gently graduate the scallops so that they fall to the sides in progressively longer lengths from a high point at the centre of the blind. This type of arrangement can look stunning on a picture window, and creates an attractive frame for the view beyond.

All manner of trimmings can also be used to decorate the blinds and complete the effect. Trim rich fabrics with fringing, and emphasize their full scallops by hanging a tassel below each vertical tape. Frills and lace will further soften the effect, while piping in a contrasting shade gives a sharper outline and is ideal for blinds in a formal setting.

▲ **Crowning glory**
This striking Austrian blind, shaped into a swag and tail arrangement, makes a superb crown for the bedroom window, giving it height and linking it to other furnishings in the room. Rosettes fixed at each end of the blind and trimmed for a perfect match, make elegant finishing touches and add interest to the heading.

◀ **Take a bow**
In this carefully co-ordinated bathroom, the bows of the wallpaper border are carried on to the blind heading, which is decorated with fabric bows in a matching shade of pink. The ribbon theme is also reflected in the fabric of the blind and frill. Decorating the heading of the blind creates a pleasing balance between it and the full swags below.

Sheer festoon blinds

The most decorative of all blinds, a festoon is ruched into soft gathers even when lowered. When raised, the fabric is swept up into swathes of fabric. Festoon blinds look striking in sheer fabrics, as the material lends itself to the vertical and horizontal gathers. This style of blind offers privacy, but lets the light filter though – a perfect alternative to a plain net curtain. For a final flourish and

▲ A festoon with a frill *The soft voile, delicately printed with flowers and butterflies, co-ordinates with the curtains. The gathers allow light to filter through but give more privacy than a sheer curtain.*

to give the edge definition, add a frill to the base edge. You can make a bold statement with a deep one or choose a narrower edging.

Positioning the track

Festoon blinds are held at the window on either a special blind curtain track or on a standard track fixed to a length of wooden battening.

The blind track carries cord holders which can be moved to a position above each length of vertical tape. A cord lock fixed at one end of the track holds the cords neatly in position, so the blind can be raised and held at any height over the window.

The standard track mounted on battening will have to have small screw eyes added to the underside of the battening above each vertical tape to hold the pulley cords.

The track or battening can be wall or ceiling mounted. In a recessed window, the track will fit inside the recess, while on a flat window, the blind can extend beyond the surround on either side to suit the décor of the room.

Cut and fit the track or battening in place at the window before working out your fabric quantities.

Fabric quantities

For the length, measure from the track to the sill and allow for one and a half times this measurement. Measure the width of the track and double this measurement. Allow extra fabric for the base frill. For example, if the frill is 8cm (3in) deep, calculate the extra fabric for a strip 10cm (4in) deep (to allow for the seams and hem) and twice the width of the blind.

Constructing the blind

The blind is composed of vertical tapes which are evenly spaced across the back of the blind. The position of the tapes will depend on the blind width. When joining fabric widths together, position the seam centrally, then cover the raw edges of the seam with the festoon blind tape. Divide the area between the outer and central tapes into equal sections and place the remaining tapes at these points – the closer the tapes, the tighter the swags. If the tapes are up to 40cm (16in) apart, for example, they will produce a wide, full swag. Further apart, the swag will be shallower.

The tapes are pulled up to fit the window depth. The blind is lowered and raised by cords threaded through the vertical tapes. The complete blind then has the addition of a heading tape which gathers up the blind horizontally into regular pencil pleats.

Festoon blind kits are available. They contain everything you need (except the fabric, thread and track or track and batten) and are available from major department stores.

MAKING THE BLIND

1 Cutting out Straighten the edge of the fabric. Cut pieces of fabric to chosen size and join any widths. The width of the blind will depend on your choice of heading tape.

3 Placing the tapes Lay the fabric wrong side up on a flat surface. Mark the position of the tapes at either side and equally spaced in between. Cut a length of festoon blind tape for each position, the same length as the fabric, with the first loop of each tape 5cm (2in) up from the end. Pin the first two vertical tapes over the side hems with the inner edge just covering the raw edge of the fabric.

2 Hem the sides Turn under a 2.5cm (1in) hem down both side edges. Pin and tack hems in place.

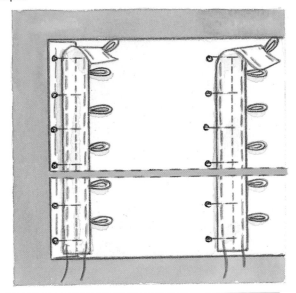

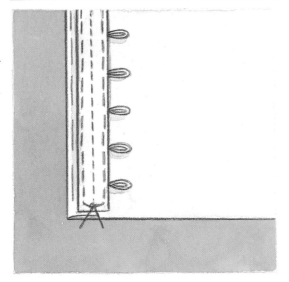

4 Stitching the tapes Draw out the ends of cords on the wrong side of the end of each tape, and knot. Place the loops towards the inside edge of the blind. Stitch in place down the centre of each tape, catching down side hems at the same time.

▼ *Festoon blind track*
Seen from the back are the curtain hooks; cord tidys for vertical tape cords, with the cord holders on the track above taking vertical cords across to the cord lock, on the left.

Materials

Blind track or length of wooden battening, screw eyes and standard curtain track.

Sheer fabric, see above for how to work out quantities.

Festoon blind tape, the length of the blind times the number of tapes.

Matching thread

Plastic rings, small curtain rings, one for each length of vertical tape.

Transparent curtain heading tape, the width of the blind.

Fine nylon cord, for each vertical tape you need twice the length plus one width of the blind.

Cleat

◀ *Pretty pink swags* A festoon blind in glazed cotton hangs in more voluptuous folds than a sheer festoon which lies flatter against the window, making it simpler to draw the curtains. These patterned, frilled curtains are tied back and it is the festoon that is used to cover the window at night.

5 Making the frill Measure the lower edge of the blind and double the measurement. For an 8cm (3in) deep frill, cut out 10cm (4in) wide strips from across the fabric width, until you have the correct length. Pin and stitch the strips together with narrow French seams into one long length.

6 Hemming the frill Turn under a double 6mm (¹/₄in) hem on lower and side edges of frill; pin and stitch in place. Work two rows of gathering stitches 6mm (¹/₄in) and 1.5cm (⁵/₈in) from the top raw edge.

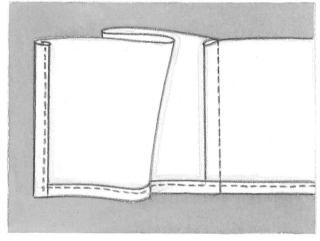

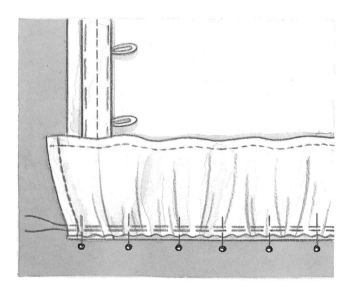

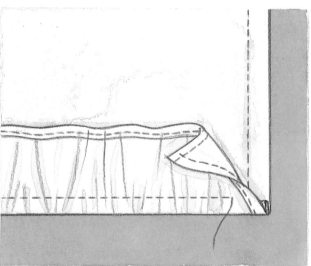

7 Stitching frill to blind Place the frill to blind with wrong sides together, pull up the gathering stitches evenly to fit the blind. Pin and stitch frill in place, 6mm (¹/₄in) from the edge, catching in ends of vertical tapes.

8 Completing French seam Re-fold with right sides together, then lightly press with seam to edge. Pin and stitch 1cm (³/₈in) from the seamed edge, to complete the French seam.

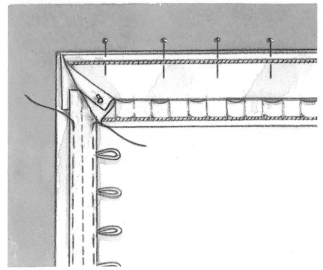

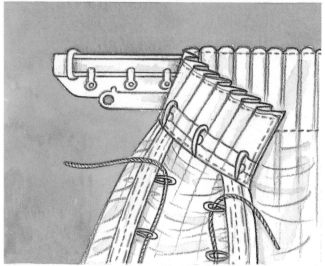

9 **Adding the heading tape** Turn down top edge of blind for width of heading tape. Trim vertical tapes so there is only 1cm (³/₈in) tucked under the edge of tape. Cut a length of heading tape to fabric width plus 2cm (³/₄in). Position tape to top folded edge. Make sure that the drawn cords on the vertical tapes are left hanging free. At one side of heading tape, pull out drawn cords from the tape and knot.

Turn under the tape end for 1cm (³/₈in) so it is in line with outer edge. At opposite side, pull out cords from the right side of the tape and leave to hang free. Turn under tape end in line with edge, as before.

10 **Stitching the heading tape** Pin and stitch heading tape in place, catching down the knotted cords at one side, but leaving hanging cords free at the opposite edge. Draw up the cords across the heading tape to fit the track. Knot surplus cords together but do not cut off. Wind up surplus cord and knot to hold.

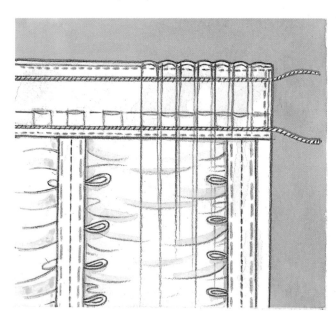

11 **Fitting blind to track** Draw up each vertical tape in turn, until blind measures the window drop. Space the gathers evenly down the whole blind. Knot cords together, but do not cut off. Wind surplus cords up and knot together to hold.

12 **Hanging the blind** Fit curtain hooks through the heading tape, evenly spaced about 8cm (3in) apart. Attach a cleat to the side of the window, near the bottom, on the same side as the cord lock on the track.

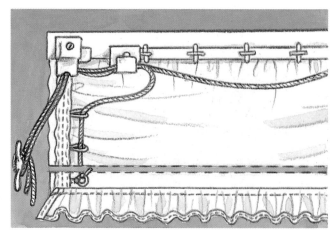

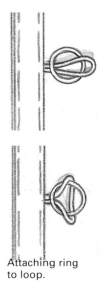

Attaching ring to loop.

13 **Cording the blind** Fasten a plastic ring into the loop at the base of each vertical tape. Insert the loop through the ring, then pull the loop round the outer rim of the ring to hold securely. Cut a length of cord for each length of vertical tape, twice the length of the blind plus one width.

Beginning at the side opposite to the cleat, knot the cord to the base ring. Thread the cord up through the loops on the tape to the top of the blind. Then take the cord through the cord holders on the track and the cord lock at the opposite side, or through the screw eyes on the battening. Repeat, to thread a length of cord through each length of vertical tape in the same way, until all the cords are hanging together at one side.

14 **Adjust the blind** Pull up the blind so it is resting on the sill and knot the cords together just beyond the cord lock, or the last of the screw eyes. Plait the cords together and knot again at sill level. Trim excess cords level. Alternatively, leave cords free and knot together at sill level. A decorative 'acorn' can be added to the ends of the cords.

Basics of curtain making

Curtains, pelmets and valances transform a room. To be really effective, they need to be planned carefully. Even using curtains on their own gives a variety of different effects, depending on the fullness and length of the curtains, the heading tape used, and the type of pole or track.

Choosing curtain track

Pick a strong enough track, lightweight for sheers and unlined cottons; medium weight for standard sill-length curtains; and heavyweight for floor-length or heavy, interlined curtains.

If the track has to go round corners, as in a bay or bow window, choose a flexible plastic track or a metal track fitted with sections which can be easily slotted together as required.

If the track is covered by a valance or pelmet, it doesn't need to be elaborate, but if the track is on display, pick one that will fit the decor and the style of the curtains.

For maximum light and to reveal the shape of the window, allow extra track at each side so the curtains can be pulled back. The amount of extra track will depend on the thickness of the curtain and the space available. Generally 15-46cm (6-18in) at each side will be sufficient.

Check that you have everything you need. Tracks are usually bought as a complete kit with screws, brackets, overlapping arms (where necessary) curtain hooks and gliders. However, there may be optional extras.

Always follow the fixing instructions supplied with the track, making sure that the end fixings are strong and that there are sufficient holding brackets in between to prevent the track from sagging. To save time, check through all the fittings first, so that you are familiar with them. If there is a concrete lintel above the window or the wall is badly plastered, the track will have to be mounted on a wooden batten fixed above the window for a level result.

◀ *Elegant window dressing*
These blue and white chintz, tailored floor-length curtains have been partnered with the full range of window dressing – boxed pelmet with a pleated valance, sheer curtains and tailored tie-backs. Piping adds a crisp finish to tie-backs and pelmet.

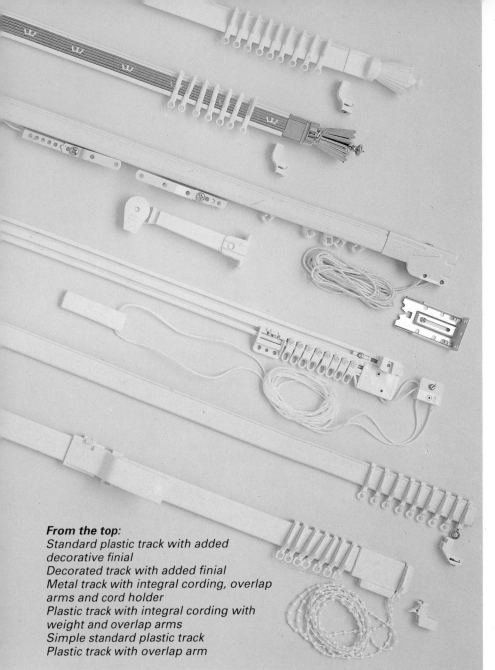

Track additions

There are several tracks available with useful extras. To hang curtains with detachable linings, you can buy a track with hooks which make it possible to remove the lining without taking down the whole curtain. For heavy curtains choose a track with integral cording, or add a cording set to it. Easier to fit are draw rods that hook into the leading runner and hang behind the curtains.

If you wish to have a valance above the curtains, consider getting a valance rail which is slotted on to the front of curtain track. There are also triple tracks to hold a blind behind the curtains, as well as a valance in front.

Heading tapes

If the length of the curtains is correct and the seams and hems are straight, the only addition needed for a beautifully tailored result is an attractive heading. With the advent of commercially made heading tapes this part of curtain making is easy. If you like, you can make beautiful pleats by hand, but for most windows an evenly pleated pencil or triple pleat gathered by heading tape is all you need.

Choosing heading tapes

Choose a type of heading tape which suits the style of the curtains and flatters the fabric. Decorative headings add interest to plain fabrics, while plainer ones with shallow pleats will show off fabrics with large prints.

From the top:
Standard plastic track with added decorative finial
Decorated track with added finial
Metal track with integral cording, overlap arms and cord holder
Plastic track with integral cording with weight and overlap arms
Simple standard plastic track
Plastic track with overlap arm

Box pleat *A formal heading tape, this will emphasize the length of the curtains. The tape automatically makes equally spaced pleats which show up best on plain fabrics. You will need fabric twice the finished curtain width.*

Cartridge pleat *A good choice for curtains in heavier fabrics or interlined curtains. Hooks should be placed at each end and behind each pleat. Match the pleats across the centre opening unless curtains overlap. You will need fabric twice the finished curtain width.*

POSITIONING THE TRACK

You can create illusions with the window proportions by positioning the track at different levels.

The tracks can be fixed either to the wall, the window frame or, if necessary, to the ceiling. If you wish to have a pelmet, you must leave space between the track and the ceiling for the brackets to be fixed.

To make a window seem longer, hang track high above the frame without much extra each side.

To give extra width, increase the space at each side.

To make a window seem larger all round, increase space at the sides and above.

Pencil pleat *Ideal for most settings, this heading tape gives an elegant look to curtains. It comes in different widths to match the curtain lengths – deeper headings to give a better proportion on longer curtains. When buying fabric you will need 2½ times the finished curtain width.*

Tudor ruff *This type of heading is a decorative alternative to the pencil pleat and is ideal for jazzing up plain fabrics. You will need fabric twice the finished curtain width.*

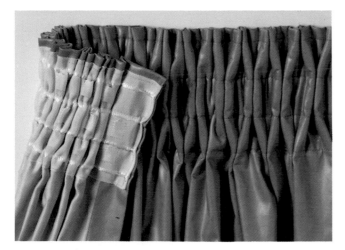

Smocked *This is extremely decorative and looks good on both plain and patterned fabrics. You will need fabric no more than twice the finished curtain width.*

Triple pleat *This heading tape drapes the fabric beautifully for a tailored look. Position the tape so that the pleats fall evenly across the curtains with equal space at each end and match pleats across the centre opening, unless curtains overlap. As for cartridge pleats, hooks should be placed behind each pleat. You will need fabric twice the finished curtain width.*

► **Dormer delight**
In an upstairs or attic bedroom with sloping ceilings, the wide windowsill dictates the window dressing. The curtain track has been placed in the window recess, on the wall above the frame, and the curtains made to sill length. If there is no room for a track in this position use a track that can be mounted on the ceiling of the recess.

Measuring up

Before measuring up for curtains, fix the track in place so that the exact height and width can be measured. The track placement will depend on the window – its shape, whether it has a recess or not or if it is a bay.

Calculating the curtain length

Once the track is in place, decide on the curtain length. Curtains usually look best reaching to the floor or sill. They can hang between sill and floor, but check the proportion in relation to the height of the ceiling first as this length can give the impression that it was a mistake.

For a really luxurious look, curtains can look effective cut extra long to drape over the floor.

Measure from the top of the track to the chosen length, using an expandable metal ruler for accuracy. For floor or sill-length curtains, deduct 1cm (³/₈in) so the curtains will sit just above the floor or sill. Then add the allowances for hems and heading.

Calculating the width

The curtain width is dictated by the length of the track and the chosen heading. Each type of heading requires a certain amount of fabric to achieve the chosen result.

Calculate fabric requirements

Measure the required length of the curtain, including allowances for hems and headings.

Measure the length of track; decide on the type of heading and how many curtain widths you need to gain this effect.

Multiply the curtain length by the number of fabric widths to find out how much fabric you need. You must allow extra for pattern matching – one pattern repeat for each fabric width other than the first one. The shop assistant will be able to give you the measurement for the pattern repeat of the fabric.

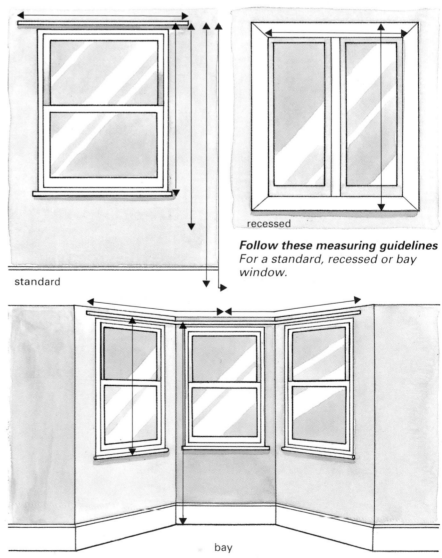

standard

recessed

Follow these measuring guidelines
For a standard, recessed or bay window.

bay

Stylish curtains

Hanging curtains at the window will instantly make a room look and feel warmer. In fact, windows without some form of dressing can look unfinished. In a plainly decorated room curtains give you the opportunity to add a splash of colour or to introduce pattern and texture. Simple, unlined curtains are no more complicated than sheers or nets, and although they look impressive, even heavy, lined curtains are not difficult to make although they do, of course, take a little longer. This chapter gives the basic techniques used in curtain making; later chapters will cover a variety of decorative treatments.

▲ A well-dressed window
These sewn-in linings are made in a colour taken from the pattern on the curtains and are displayed when the curtains are held back. The same fabric is used to add box pleated frills to the valance and tie-backs, completing the co-ordinated effect.

Whether to add lining

For summer use or in kitchens, bathrooms and stairways, simple unlined curtains are all you need. They provide some privacy without obscuring all the natural light. The finer and lighter in colour the fabric, the more light will be able to pass through.

However, if using an expensive fabric, or when making curtains for warmth or privacy, it is important to add a lining. This increases the insulation, cuts out light and protects the fabric from the damaging effects of dust and sunlight. It also improves the hang of the curtains by adding body and weight, giving them a more tailored look, which is ideal for bedrooms and living rooms.

For best results the lining should be of good quality and suitable for the fabric weight, so that it wears as well as the curtain. Choose a lining in a matching or toning colour, or go for traditional white or beige. If choosing a darker or contrasting colour, take a scrap of the main fabric with you when you buy, since coloured linings can show through paler curtain fabrics.

Lining methods

Detachable lining A detachable lining is attached to the curtain with curtain hooks, and can easily be removed for washing or during the summer months. It can be added to an existing unlined curtain, and is an ideal choice for difficult fabrics, since the lining and curtain can be cleaned separately. In addition, it does not need to be gathered as much as the main curtain, which means a saving on fabric.

Sewn-in lining This is literally sewn into the curtain while it is being made, and cannot be detached for washing. It gives good results quickly, and helps to support the main fabric. Unless the curtain and lining have the same care properties, the finished curtain must be dry cleaned or the fabrics may shrink at different rates.

Types of lining

Cotton sateen is a tightly woven, hard-wearing fabric, available in a variety of colours. It is the most readily available lining fabric and comes in two standard widths, 122cm (48in) and 138cm (54in).

Thermal sateen feels like standard cotton sateen, but has been coated to give it insulating properties. It contains a mixture of cotton and synthetic fibres.

Milium lining is a cotton sateen which has been coated on one side with a solution of aluminium particles giving it a silvery appearance. The silvery side should be placed up against the wrong side of the fabric to reflect heat back into the room. Its insulating qualities mean that in hot weather it will also help to keep heat out if the curtains are drawn during the day.

Blackout lining is thick, heavy and usually beige coloured. It has all the properties of thermal lining but will also keep out the light, making it ideal for people who are easily woken by light. It will also help to dampen noise from

▼ **Simple but effective**
These unlined curtains are hung on the pole using hooks threaded through ungathered standard heading tape.

92

UNLINED CURTAINS

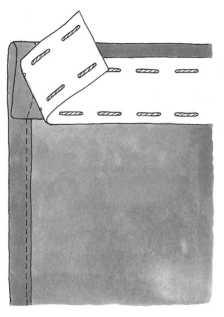

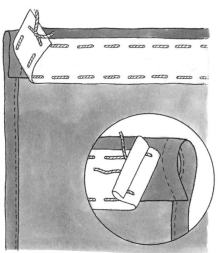

1 Measuring up Measure the drop from the curtain rail to the finished curtain length and add extra for heading and hem allowances. Usually 20cm (8in) extra is sufficient. Calculate the number of fabric widths you need for each curtain – generally twice the finished curtain width. Then multiply the length by the number of widths. For each additional fabric width you will need to add one pattern repeat for pattern matching.

2 Cutting out For accuracy, straighten the fabric edge before cutting out as many fabric widths as required. Match patterns if necessary, then stitch together with French seams, positioning any cut edges at the outer edge of each curtain. If using the selvedges, snip into them at 10-15cm (4-6in) intervals, to prevent puckering.

3 Stitch side hems Turn under 5mm (¼in) then 2cm (¾in) to wrong side along both sides. Slipstitch or machine stitch in place.

4 Fold top hem Turn down the top edge of the fabric by the depth of the tape plus 5mm (¼in) for stand heading. Cut a length of heading tape the width of the curtain fabric plus 2cm (¾in). Place the heading tape, 1cm (⅜in) from the folded edge, over the top raw edge of the fabric; trim fabric edge if necessary and pin.

5 Neaten heading tape ends At the leading edge of the curtain (where the curtains meet), pull out the heading tape cords from the *wrong* side of the tape; knot. Turn under edge of tape by 1cm (⅜in) and position against the edge of the curtain.

On the outer edge, pull out the heading tape cords from the *right* side of the tape. Turn under the edge of tape by 1cm (⅜in) and place against the curtain edge.

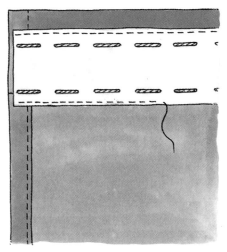

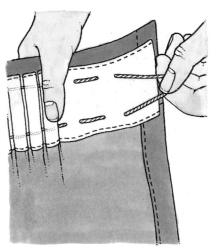

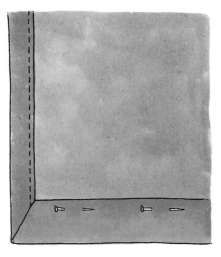

6 Stitch heading tape Pin, tack and stitch heading tape in place along the marked line on each long edge of the tape. Stitch both rows in the same direction to prevent puckering.

7 Gather the curtain Pull up the heading tape cords from the outer edge until the curtain is the correct width; knot and trim ends or wind surplus cords on to a cord tidy. Hook the tidy into the heading tape.

8 Stitch lower hem Hang the curtain to check its length. Remove and turn up a double hem along the lower edge. To mitre the corners, fold the bottom hem allowance under at an angle at the corner until its top edge touches the side hem allowance. Slipstitch corners and bottom hem.

Working with patterned fabric
If you find that a large pattern has been printed slightly off grain, cut out the fabric widths following the pattern and not the grain. When cutting out the fabric widths, always position the complete pattern along the base hem edge. Any cut pattern at the top will be lost in the gathers of the heading.

To join widths together, match the pattern on the right side and tack with ladder stitch. Work from the right side of the fabric as shown right. Machine stitch in the usual way close to the tacking. Remove tacking.

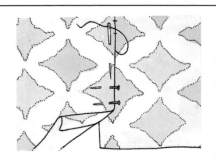

DETACHABLE LININGS

1 **Making the curtain** Make up the curtain in the same way as an unlined curtain, with 2cm (³/₄in) side hems and 8cm (3¹/₄in) base hems.

2 **Making the lining** Detachable linings only need to be one and a half to twice the track length. Make up the lining in the same way, but 2.5cm (1in) shorter than the curtain.

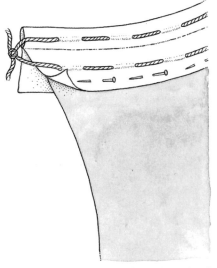

3 **Apply lining tape** Cut a length of lining tape the width of the lining, plus 2cm (³/₄in). Slot over the top of the fabric and pin. Tie the cords as for the main curtain. Fold under 5mm (¹/₄in) at each end of the tape and stitch. Stitch the tape to the lining along the lower edge of the tape.

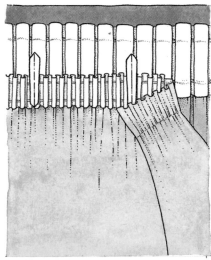

4 **Hang the curtain** Pull up both curtain and lining the required amount, so they match. Slot each hook through the lining tape, then the curtain tape and on to the track. Check the length of the lining, then remove and make a double hem.

SEWN-IN LININGS

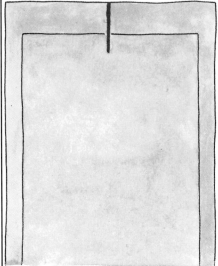

1 **Cutting out** Measure up and cut out the fabric for the curtain, joining widths together as necessary. Cut and stitch the lining in the same way to make a panel 8cm (3in) shorter and 4cm (1¹/₂in) narrower than the curtain. Do not tear lining fabrics, but use a T-square or set square and ruler to provide a straight edge. Mark the centre of both fabric and lining.

2 **Stitch side edges** Place the curtain to the lining, right sides together, matching side edges and with top edges level. Pin, tack and machine stitch side edges, taking 1.5cm (⁵/₈in) seam allowances and stitching from the top to within 18cm (7in) of the lower edge.

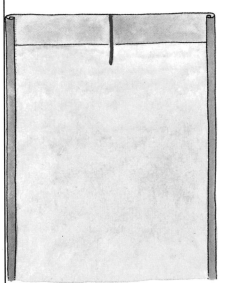

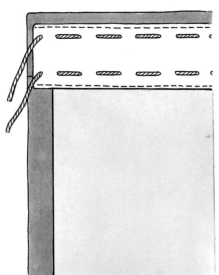

3 **Turn right side out** Turn curtain and lining through to the right side. Match the centre of the curtain to the centre of the lining and press. A 2cm (³/₄in) wide border of curtain fabric will form down the sides edges.

4 **Apply heading tape** Treating the lining and fabric as one along the top, turn down the top edge of the curtain by the depth of the heading tape and stand. Apply heading tape in the same way as for an unlined curtain, above.

5 **Hem the lining** Hang the curtain at the window to check its length. Turn up a double 2.5cm (1in) hem along base edge of lining so that the lining will hang 2.5cm (1in) above the finished curtain; pin or tack and machine stitch.

6 **Hem the curtain** Turn up a double 5cm (2in) hem along the lower edge of the curtain. Mitre the corners as in step 8 for an unlined curtain. At the lower side edges, slipstitch the lining to the curtains.

Curtains with a flourish

A frill is the final flourish which transforms a simple pair of curtains into something really special. It gives the curtains a freshness and softness which epitomises the country style, and provides that extra detail which is the mark of professionally made curtains.

The frill can be used to introduce a new colour into the room, as in the picture above, or perhaps to link in with the colours of other soft furnishings used. This is done by making the frill in a different colour, or by the use of an appropriate trimming. You can trim a single frill by binding the edge, or a double frill by separating it from the main curtain with a line of piping or a smaller, contrasting or toning frill. If using tiebacks, these should be trimmed to match.

▲ Prettily edged in pink
A frill edged with pink piping has a soft and warming effect on pale mint curtains chosen to blend in with the walls of the bathroom. Adding a clever touch, the binding has been stitched to the centre of the tie-backs to complete the look.

Adding a frill

A frill can be added to the leading edges (the centre edges of a pair of curtains), to the leading and lower edges, or to both the side and lower edges. Choose to add either a single or double frill, depending on the type of fabric you have and the style you wish to achieve.

Single frills These are mainly used on unlined curtains and are made from a single layer of fabric which gathers easily. The outside edge of the frill is finished neatly either with a double hem or pretty contrast binding. A single frill requires less fabric than a double frill, making it more economical. However, the light usually shows through a single frill, so where the main curtain is lined this may not look appropriate.

Double frills Mainly used on lined curtains, these are made from a wide strip of fabric, folded lengthways, so that the fold is on the outside edge. The fold gives a smooth, crisp finish, and the extra fabric gives the frill more body. If using very heavy fabrics, such as velvet or tapestry, use a lightweight lining fabric on the back of the frill instead of doubling the fabric to give less bulk.

Frill widths Depends on the weight of the fabric, the size of the curtain and whether it is double or single. As a guide the finished width should be between 5 and 10cm (2–4in).

UNLINED CURTAIN WITH SINGLE FRILL

1 Measure and cut out Decide on the finished width of the frill – 4-10cm (1½-4in) is usual. Add 3cm (1in) for seam allowances and cut out strips to this width across the fabric, from selvedge to selvedge. Trim off the selvedges, and using narrow French seams, join the strips to make one piece twice the length of all the edges to be frilled.

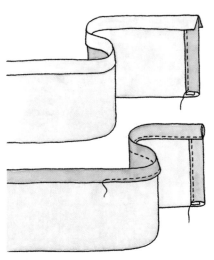

2 Neaten edges Turn under 1cm (³/₈in), then another 1cm (³/₈in) to make a narrow double hem at the two ends. Bind the long outside edge, or turn a double 1cm (³/₈in) hem.

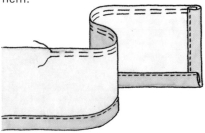

3 Gather up Sew two rows of gathering stitches along the raw edge of the frill, working in sections of up to about 80cm (31½in) to keep the thread a manageable length.

4 Cut out the curtain Cut out and join the curtain fabric widths to the required size, remembering to allow for the frill depth when calculating the finished dimensions.

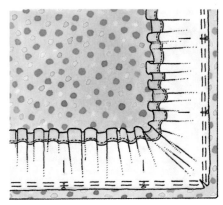

5 Pin frill to curtain Position the frill on the main fabric, right sides together. Match the hemmed ends of the frill to the position of the finished edges at the top of the curtain. Pull up gathers evenly to fit, allowing extra gathers at the corners for ease. Check the arrangement of gathers, pin and tack. Snip into seam allowance of frill at corner. Tack and stitch the frill to the curtain. Neaten seam allowances.

6 Finish curtain Fold over the top of the curtain and attach the heading tape of your choice in the usual way (see page 88).

▶ *The bottom line*
A frill along the bottom edge of the curtains adds length, allowing the curtains to billow on to the sill. The tie-backs, positioned high up, complete the illusion to make a fairly small window look longer.

LINED CURTAIN WITH DOUBLE FRILL

1 **Measure and cut out** Decide on the finished width of the frill, double it, and add 1.5cm (⅝in) for the seam allowance. Cut out and join strips as for a single frill to make up a strip twice the length of all the edges to be frilled.

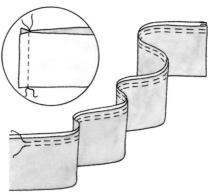

2 **Prepare frill** Fold the frill in half along its length, right sides together, and pin together at ends. Press and stitch a narrow seam at each end. Turn right side out, press and stitch two rows of gathering stitches along the raw edges, working in sections as for single frill.

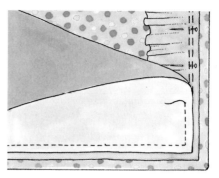

3 **Gather and attach** Gather frill and pin to the right side of the curtain, allowing extra ease at the corner for turning, and tack in place. Place the lining on the main fabric, right sides together, matching all edges. Pin and stitch sides and bottom, taking a 1.5cm (⅝in) seam. Trim and turn through to the right side. Attach heading tape.

▼ Frills with everything
A frilled trio of curtains made from light and airy cotton fabric and lined to improve the hang. The double frill stands up crisply.

▲ New nets from old
Co-ordinate your existing net curtains with a new bedspread or duvet cover by attaching matching fabric frills to the curtains. The curtains will look like new.

▶ Lovely lace
A wide lace edging makes an attractive trimming on a set of curtains, and is quick to attach since both edges of the lace are already finished. Piping is optional.

◀ Bound to succeed
A strip of fabric bound on both edges has been gathered in the middle to make an unusual curtain frill. The tie-backs and rosette are bound to match, and the wide, padded binding on the top of the curtain completes the effect.

▶In contrast
A pale blue chintz frill, used to trim a patterned curtain over an archway, is a clever link with the blue of the wallpaper and the woodwork.

Elegant curtain tiebacks

By catching the curtains back at just the right height, tiebacks pull the curtain fabric into an attractive sweep and allow natural light into the room. Wide, full curtains drape into deep scoops of fabric, while narrow drapes are given an elegant form when tied back against the frame. Don't feel that you are forced to choose one style or another by the width of the window – a large curtain swept to one side can be just as effective as the more usual set of curtains pulled back either side.

Easy to make and economical – you only need a small amount of the original curtain fabric or a remnant in a toning material – tiebacks can be made up in a variety of shapes and styles to suit any window in the home. Formal, curved tiebacks made from fabric and stiffened with heavyweight interfacing or buckram are the usual style, but softer shapes of plaited, frilled or ruched fabric are also attractive, particularly where the tone of the room is softer.

▲ **Floral arrangement**
The large floral fabric used to make these summer curtains has been carefully positioned on the tieback so that the main floral motif is shown to best effect. On a pair of tiebacks, arrange the motifs so that the tiebacks make a symmetrical pair.

Positioning tiebacks

On sill-length curtains the tiebacks are usually positioned about two-thirds of the way down from the top of the curtain, but on longer curtains and floor-length curtains there is more scope for choosing your own position. Each position has its own effect on the look of the window, so choose carefully.

In general, the lower the tieback, the fuller the effect of the curtains but the more the view and the natural light are obscured. If the view is not particularly special or the window frame is unattractive or needs some work done on it, this can be an advantage. Try different positions, draping the fabric in a gentle curve or a fuller sweep.

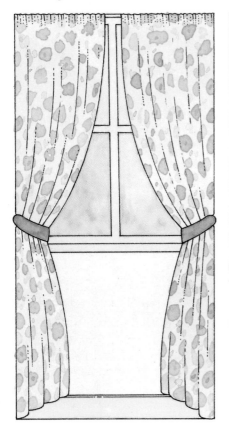

Sill length tiebacks On long, floor-length curtains the sill can be about midway down the curtain. It allows the fabric to sweep into a generous curve above the tieback and drape elegantly below it.

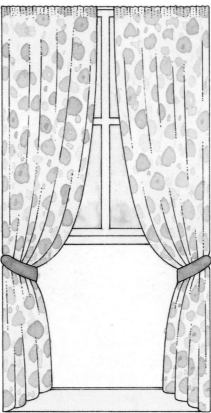

Placed low Tiebacks set about two-thirds of the way down the curtain create a full effect that can make a narrow window seem wider. But the curtains cover more of the window, and this will obscure light.

Placed high Positioned one-third of the way down from the top of the curtain, the tiebacks will give the impression of length and will let in maximum light.

Selecting the fabric

Pick a mediumweight fabric, such as a closely-woven furnishing fabric for the tieback, using the same fabric on both sides, or selecting a matching or toning lining fabric for the back. If making them in the same fabric as the curtains, bind the edges with bias binding to give the tiebacks definition. Alternatively go for a contrast, to add a dash of colour to a plain window dressing or perhaps to pick up the colours of a rug, tablecloth or sofa.

When adding tiebacks to a pair of existing curtains you may not be able to find more of the original fabric, which may, in any case, have faded. In this situation it's best to go for a contrast which will look far better than a fabric that falls just short of matching the original window dressing.

Drape the fabric round the curtain to judge the effect, or if you only have a sample of fabric, pin it to the curtains and leave it there for a few days before you make your final choice. Check it in daylight as well as in the glow of artificial light.

Positioning the fabric

The tiebacks use only a small amount of fabric, but because they are an important element of the window decoration, and because they are often quite eye catching, it is important to arrange the fabric carefully. Move the pattern around on the fabric to see what sort of arrangement you can achieve.

If the fabric is patterned with separate motifs, look for a particularly attractive detail which would fit nicely into the tieback shape. If the motif faces in a particular direction, such as a bird or animal motif, try to get it facing towards the centre of the tieback, so that in the

Tieback tie in
When you wish to change a room's colour scheme, and the curtains don't quite tie in, make tiebacks in the new colour to act as a link. A simple trimming sewn to the leading edge of the curtains will complete the effect.

finished arrangement it will be facing the window, drawing the eye in this direction.

On a pair of curtains, a symmetrical arrangement looks best, rather than an identical pair.

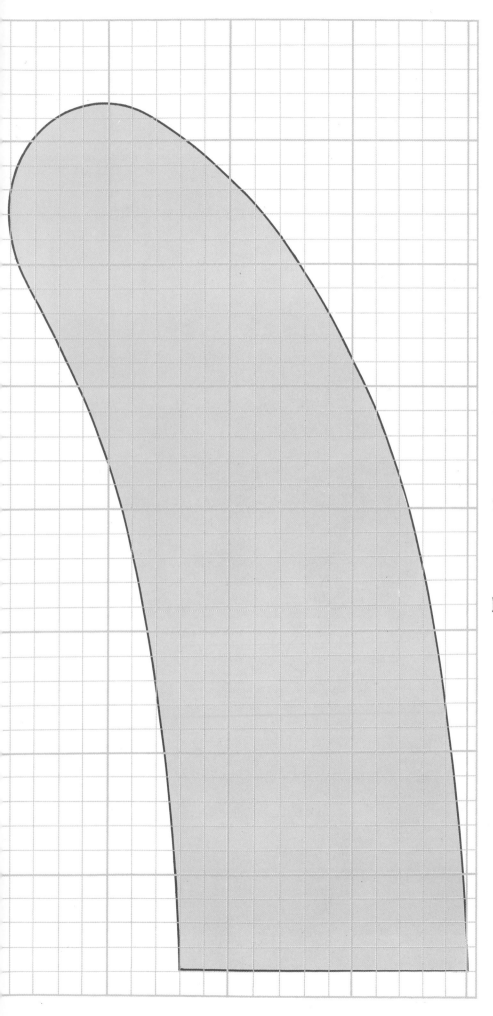

◀ *Tieback pattern*
On squared paper, draw up the pattern for the tieback from the grid so that each large square equals 5cm (2in). For quicker and more accurate results, use a photocopier to enlarge the pattern by 160% to full size.

A TAILORED TIEBACK

The pattern given here is for a standard tieback 10cm (4in) wide and 35.5cm (14in) long. Try out the effect by positioning your paper pattern on the curtain. On large curtains you may wish to widen or lengthen it.

Materials
Mediumweight fabric
Buckram or **heavyweight interfacing**
Two curtains rings per tieback
Matching thread

1 Positioning Hold a tape measure round the curtain, pulling it back, and sliding it up and down to find the best position for the tieback. Mark the wall where your head is. Ease out the fabric to create a draped effect, and read off the length on the tape measure; this will be the length of the finished tieback.

2 Making the pattern Fold a large sheet of paper or newspaper in half and draw up the tieback pattern from the diagram with the straight edge on the fold. If you wish to alter it, do so now, lengthening or shortening along the straight edge. Cut out the pattern and unfold the paper. Test the paper pattern by pinning it in place round the curtain.

3 Cutting out For each tieback cut out one piece of heavyweight interfacing or buckram to size. Cut out two pieces of fabric or one piece of fabric and one of lining, adding 1.5cm (⅝in) seam allowance all round the pattern.

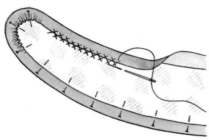

4 Attaching the front piece
Position the interfacing centrally on the wrong side of the front piece and pin. Fold the seam allowance over the interfacing, snipping so it lies flat. Pin and then stitch with herringbone stitch.

To sew herringbone stitch, take a small stitch in the fabric, cross to the interfacing and take a small backstitch, catching the interfacing, but not the fabric. Cross back to the fabric and take a small backstitch through fabric and interfacing. Keep stitching until you have gone all the way round. The stitches should be not show on the right side.

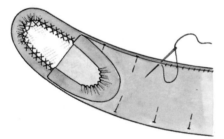

5 Attaching the back piece Turn the seam allowance of the lining to the wrong side. Place the back piece wrong side down on the interfacing and pin to hold. With small slipstitches, hand stitch all round to attach the back to the front.

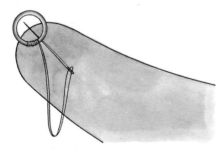

6 Attaching the rings Place a small curtain ring at each end of the tieback, so that it just overlaps the edge on the wrong side. Hand sew in place with a few straight stitches using double thread. Check the position of the tieback again by holding it in place. Then attach a small hook to the wall to hang the tiebacks from.

▲ Soft but stylish
A pale fabric used to bind this tieback softens the edges, giving the whole effect a look of comfortable luxury. For sharp definition use a darker colour from the fabric.

BOUND TIEBACK

Use the same pattern for a piped tieback as for a plain one. Bias binding is the only additional material required.

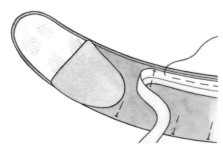

1 Cut out and pin Cut two pieces of fabric and one piece of interfacing for each tieback. Sandwich the interfacing between the fabric, wrong sides together, and pin. Tack the binding to the tieback, right sides together, with the join in the binding at one end. Snip into the seam allowance of the binding to ease round curves.

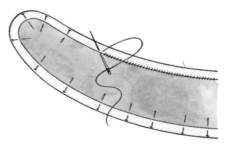

2 Stitch together Stitch the bias binding to the tieback, then press it over the edge of the tieback, and turn under the binding seam allowance level with the previous stitching line. Slipstitch the binding in place, then sew a ring to each end of the tieback as in step 6 for a tailored tieback, shown left.

Fancy curtain ties

Pretty or bold, subtle or elegant, flamboyant or formal, tiebacks can be used to enhance almost any curtain arrangement. Stiffened and tailored tiebacks are fine for formal effects, but for the softer look of the country style, why not opt for something really special. You will be surprised at the variety of attractive tieback effects you can achieve with a remnant of fabric and the minimum of sewing skills.

Soft tieback styles

There are many tieback styles to choose from, as simple or as complex as you like. Here is a selection to choose from.

Tieback bows can be made either from just one fabric, or with a backing or trimming in another colour – perhaps the colour of the curtain lining. For a soft effect the bows are unstiffened, but for a firmer, more structured look they can be stiffened with a light interfacing. The bows are attached in the desired position on a tailored or bound tieback.

Frilled tiebacks are a pretty idea for feminine room settings or for where the curtain or valance are also frilled.

Gathered tiebacks have the sophisticated look of a tailored tieback, but greater decorative interest. The tieback can be gathered or pleated by hand, but for quick results simply gather it up with curtain tape.

Plaited tiebacks can be made from just one fabric or up to three, depending on

▲ Frilled ensemble
Where the curtains and valance have a frilled edge, a frilled tieback is the final touch to complete the ensemble. The frill is narrower on the tieback than on the curtain since a wide frill would look too fussy on such a small item.

your colour scheme, and are much easier to make than they look. The secret is to pad the fabric strips which adds body and gives a more luxurious effect. This can be done by using kapok to stuff the fabric, but for a softer and more even effect you may find it easier to use a strip of lightweight wadding.

FRILLED TIEBACKS

1 Cutting out Cut out the tieback front and back pieces as for a tailored tieback, adding 1.5cm (⅝in) seem allowances all round (see page 101). Cut out a frill piece one and a half times the length of the front by 16cm (6¼in), joining pieces if necessary. Finally cut out a piece of heavy interfacing from the tieback pattern, omitting seam allowances

2 Making the frill Fold the frill in half lengthways with wrong sides together and pin and then stitch seams at each end. Trim seam allowances, turn right side out and press. Run a line of gathering threads 1 and 2cm (⅜ and ⅞in) from the raw edge through both layers along the length of the frill.

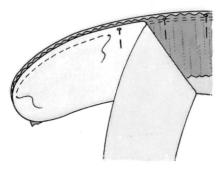

3 Attaching the frill Pull up the gathering threads on the frill so that it is the same length as the tieback piece. Tack to the lower edge of the front piece, right sides together. Place the back piece right side down on top, pin and then stitch the seam along the lower edge of the tieback, enclosing the frill. Remove the tacking threads.

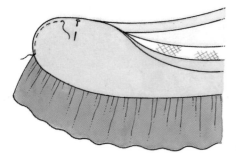

4 Finishing off Turn the tieback right side out and slip the interfacing inside. Fold the seam allowances of the front piece under, enclosing the interfacing and tack. Turn under the seam allowances of the back piece to match and tack. Working from the right side, topstitch close to the edge starting at the frill and going up one side, across the top and down to the frill on the other side. Attach a curtain ring to the wrong side at each end.

GATHERED TIEBACKS

1 Cutting out Calculate the finished length of the tieback as in step 1 above. The length of the front and back pieces depend on the type of heading tape you choose. If the tape requires twice the fabric length to gather correctly, cut out two pieces the width of the tape plus 2cm (¾in) x twice the finished length of the tieback plus 2cm (¾in). Cut the tape the same length.

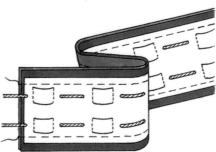

2 Stitching the seams Place the front and back together, right sides facing, and centre the tape on top. Pull out the cords from the tape at one end and fold under. Starting at the other end, stitch along one long edge, down the end, stitching across the cords, then stitch the other long edge, leaving one end free.

▲ Even results
This type of gathered tieback is perhaps the easiest of all to make. Curtain tape, the same width as the finished tieback, is used to achieve even gathers.

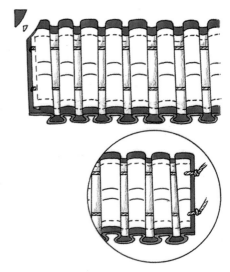

3 Completing the tiebacks Pull up the cord in the tape from the free end to gather and then knot to secure; snip off excess cord. Trim the corners and turn right side out. Tuck seam allowances inside at the free end, slipstitch closed and then attach a curtain ring at each end.

BOW TIEBACKS

1 Making the tieback Tie a measuring tape loosely around the curtain at the desired height to estimate the finished length of each tieback. Cut out and stitch the tieback, making it either tailored or with bound edges (see pages 99-102).

2 Cutting out the bows For each bow cut a rectangle twice the finished width plus 3cm (1¼in) for seam allowances x the full width of the fabric. If you wish to make the bow longer, join two strips of fabric with a seam at the centre.

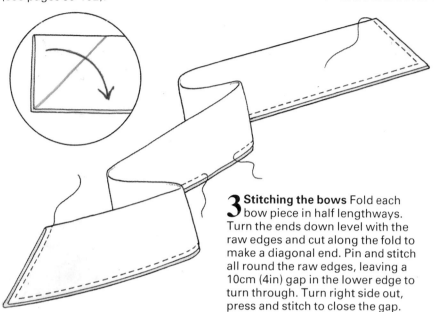

4 Finishing off Tie a bow, position the tieback at the window and arrange the bow in place in the most attractive position. Mark the tieback with tailor's chalk where the bow should go. Stitch the bow in position with a double thread in the same colour as the tieback.

▼ Bound effect
These tieback bows look like they have a bound edge, but in fact this effect is achieved by cutting the back piece larger than the front. The seam allowances on both pieces are pressed to the wrong side, and then the pieces slipstitched together.

3 Stitching the bows Fold each bow piece in half lengthways. Turn the ends down level with the raw edges and cut along the fold to make a diagonal end. Pin and stitch all round the raw edges, leaving a 10cm (4in) gap in the lower edge to turn through. Turn right side out, press and stitch to close the gap.

MAKING PLAITED TIEBACKS

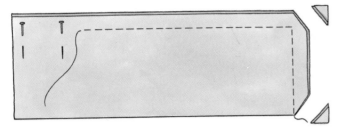

1 Making the tubes Decide on the required length of the tiebacks. For each tieback you will need three strips of fabric one and a half times the finished length x 9cm (3½in). Fold each strip in half lengthways with right sides together, pin and stitch a 1cm (⅜in) seam across one end and along the long edge to make a tube. Trim seam allowances at corners.

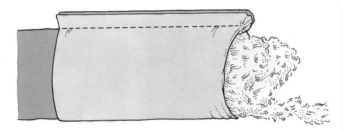

2 Stuffing the tubes Turn the tubes right side out little by little, starting at the stitched end and stuffing lightly with a strip of wadding or small amounts of kapok as you push the fabric through. When you reach the other end, pin closed.

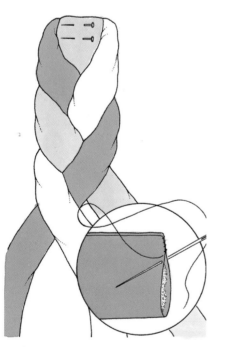 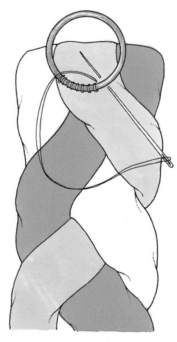

3 Checking the length Pin the three tubes together at the stitched ends and plait to check stuffing levels are correct. Check the length, and trim the tubes as necessary, remembering to add seam allowances to the trimmed ends. Separate the tubes and adjust the amount of stuffing in each one as required. Tuck seam allowances in and stitch the pinned ends closed.

4 Finishing off Pin the tubes together at one end and then stitch securely with small hand stitches. Plait the tubes and then stitch the other ends together. Sew a curtain ring on the wrong side at each end to finish.

▲ Hand-crafted
Plaited tiebacks, like wicker baskets and plaited rag rugs are very much in the country style because they look hand crafted. They work particularly well with wide curtains, such as those used over doors, since they look good even when very long.

tip

Covered cord
If you find it too fiddly to stuff the tubes with wadding or kapok, use covered cord for the plaits instead. Buy the thickest cord you can find, and cut the fabric strips 2cm (¾in) wider than the measurement round the cord. For quick coverage, cut the cord twice as long as the fabric. Wrap the fabric round it, right sides together, and stitch along the edge of the cord with a zip foot. Slide the fabric over itself on to the uncovered cord, turning it right side out. Trim off the excess cord.

Bordered curtains

A border, whether it is made from binding, lace, ribbon or fabric, can transform a simple curtain and take it above the ordinary look of standard, ready-made curtains. In a toning colour it has a subtle effect, adding definition to the shape of the curtains and, perhaps, linking in with a second colour used in the room. In a country pattern it will add decorative interest as well as definition, particularly where the main fabric is plain; while in a bold contrast colour it will add drama, drawing attention to the window.

Although borders can be added to finished or ready-made curtains, they should not be considered as a mere afterthought. When planning the whole style of the window dressing – the size of each curtain, the type of heading, and whether to have a valance, pelmet or tiebacks – the option of borders should also be considered.

By adding a wide border, you may be able to get away with using less of the main fabric, since the border can add valuable width to your curtains. This could mean the difference between using

▲ Bold border
A wide, black border adds drama to a pair of short kitchen curtains and forms a link with the new black kitchen chairs.

a favourite, but pricy fabric, and opting for a compromise from a cheaper price bracket.

The method for making this type of curtain can also be used to adapt existing curtains to fit larger windows when you move house.

107

Types of border

Double border for neat and professional results. This border is made from lengths of fabric, mitred at the corners and stitched to the main fabric so that the curtain sits neatly inside the border 'frame'.

Mock border for quick results. Ribbon or a strip of neatened fabric is stitched in place on the front of the curtain.

Lining border for curtains with attractive linings. The lining is cut larger than the curtain all round, and the excess fabric folded over to the right side of the main fabric to form the border.

There are several ways of positioning the border; it can go all round the curtain; down both sides and across the bottom, or only down the leading edge of the curtain and across the bottom. If the lower edge of the curtain is obscured by furniture or by items on the window sill, this edge can be left without a border.

◀ *Finishing line*
A three-sided border in a cheerful yellow fabric gives a neat and attractive finish to a very pretty bedroom curtain.

THREE-SIDED DOUBLE BORDER

A double border can be added to lined or unlined curtains, and is usually attached to both sides and the lower edge of the curtain. The border is cut in three sections, which are then stitched together to make the neat mitred corners, and attached to the curtain. The method requires very careful cutting and stitching and is more economical to make from plain fabrics because you don't need to worry about the direction of the pattern.

1 Assembling the curtain fabrics Cut and join the curtain fabric and lining (optional) to the required finished size plus the heading allowance. There is no need to add seam allowances to the edges where the border will go. Place the fabric on the lining, wrong sides together with all edges matching. Pin and tack together all round.

2 Cutting the border Decide on the finished width of the border – this will depend on the size of the curtain and the effect you want. Double this measurement and add 3cm (1¼in) for the seam allowances. Cut three strips this wide. Two of them, for the sides, should be the finished length of the curtain and heading plus 3cm (1¼in). The other, for the base edge, should be the finished width of the curtain plus 3cm (1¼in).

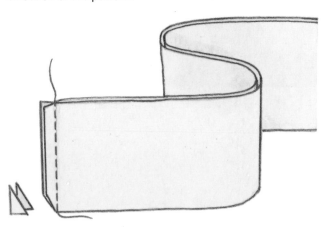

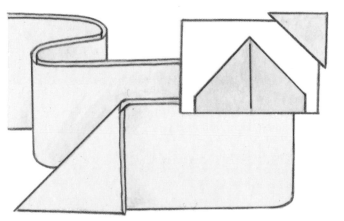

3 Preparing the side pieces Fold each side border piece in half lengthways, with right sides together. At the end which will be at the top of the curtain, stitch a 1.5cm (⅝in) seam. Trim the seam allowance at the corner and turn right side out. Press in half lengthways, this time with wrong sides together.

4 Cutting mitred corners Fold the base piece in half lengthways, wrong sides together, and press. At each end turn up the raw edges diagonally to match the fold and press. Unfold and cut along the diagonal foldlines. Repeat to cut the lower end of each of the two side border pieces.

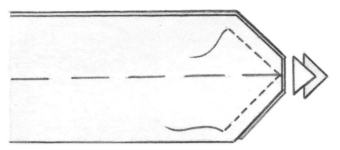

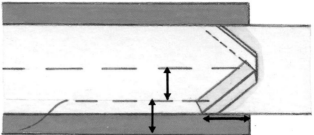

5 **Stitching the mitres** With right sides together, place one mitred end of the base piece to one of the side border pieces. Pin and stitch round the pointed edges, taking a 1.5cm (⅝in) seam and leaving 1.5cm (⅝in) free at each end of the seam. Trim off the point in the seam allowance and turn right sides out. Repeat to stitch a mitre at the other end of the base piece. Fold the fabric in half lengthways to form a frame and press along the fold.

6 **Attaching the lower border** Unfold the border and pin the lower edge of the bottom piece to the curtain with right sides together, the depth of the border minus the 1.5cm (⅝in) seam allowance from the lower edge. The arrows show the finished width of the border. Open out the seam allowances of the lower half of the mitre; tack and then stitch the border to the curtain, taking a 1.5cm (⅝in) seam allowance on the border, and stitching exactly to the mitre seam.

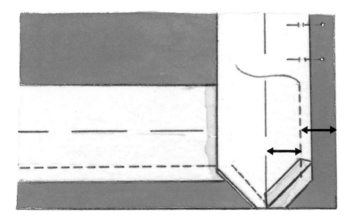

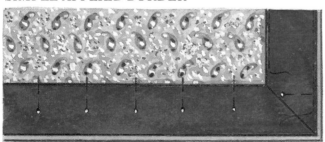

7 **Attaching the side borders** Turn each side border up, positioning it the depth of the border minus 1.5cm (⅝in) from the edge of the curtain (arrows show finished border width). The top of the border should be level with the position of the finished top edge of the curtain. Open out the seam allowance on the mitre, and taking a 1.5cm (⅝in) seam allowance on the border, pin, tack and then stitch from the top of the curtain to the mitre seam on one side of the curtain, and from the mitre seam to the top of the curtain on the other side.

8 **Finishing off** Turn the border over to the wrong/lining side of the curtain. Tuck the raw edge of the border under, and slipstitch to the curtain over the previous line of machine stitching. Turn down the top edge of the curtain, and attach the heading tape, rings or ribbons to fix the curtain to the pole or track.

SIMPLE APPLIED BORDER

A quick way to achieve a bordered effect is to use wide ribbon or a strip of fabric hemmed on each long edge and then stitched to the curtain. If the curtain is unlined, press the raw edges of the curtain to the right side first, pin the border on top, close to the folded edge, and topstitch along both long edges of the border, enclosing the raw edges. At the corners, fold the ribbon diagonally to make a quick mitre, slipstitching across the mitred fold. If the curtain is lined, attach the border the width of the seam allowance from the edges on the right side of the main fabric, and then attach the lining in the usual way to complete the curtain.

tip

Adding width
Use a border to add width to a curtain, by stitching it to the curtain only a seam allowance away from the edge, instead of inserting the curtain fully into the border. Before cutting out, calculate the finished size of the curtain exactly, taking into account the extra added by the border; then cut out the border pieces as in step 1, of the three sided double border, and continue to make the curtain in the same way, stitching the border only 1.5cm (⅝in) from the fabric edge in steps 6 and 7.

MAKING A LINING BORDER

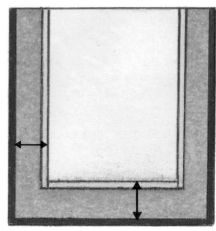

Three-sided border
Lining fabric:

width = finished curtain width
           plus 2 x border width
           plus 2 x seam allowance
length = finished curtain length
           plus 1 x border width
           plus heading allowance
           plus 1 x seam allowance

Curtain fabric:

width = width of lining
           minus 4 x border width
length = length of lining
           minus 2 x border width

Side and lower border
Lining fabric:

width = finished curtain width
           plus 1 x border width
           plus 2 x seam allowance
length = finished curtain length
           plus 1 x border width
           plus heading allowance
           plus 1 x seam allowance

Curtain fabric

width = width of lining
           minus 2 x border width
length = length of lining
           minus 2 x border width

Leading edge border
Lining fabric:

width = finished curtain width
           plus 1 x border width
           plus 2 x seam allowance
length = finished curtain length
           plus heading allowance
           plus hem allowance

Curtain fabric:

width = width of lining
           minus 2 x border width
length = length of lining

1 **Cutting out** Cut out the main fabric and lining using one of the diagrams above, depending on where you wish to add the border.

2 **Stitching the seams** Matching raw edges and with right sides together, stitch the lining to the curtain along each side edge, taking a 1.5cm (⅝in) seam allowance; turn right side out and press in position, with centres matching. The extra width of the lining will form a border on the side edges.

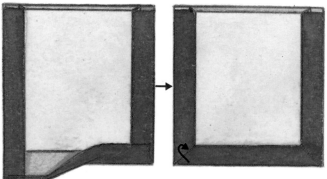

3 **Lower border** If there is a border on the bottom, turn the 1.5cm (⅝in) seam allowance to the right side, and then turn the fabric up again by the depth of the border; pin. At each corner, fold the fabric under at an angle to make a mock mitre, trimming off the excess fabric to reduce bulk. Stitch the hem, taking a few stitches into the mitred corner to secure. Attach the heading tape to complete.

◄ *Taking a lead The border down the leading edge is the same colour as the casing at the top used to hang these colourful curtains.*

Tab headings for curtains

Traditional heading tapes are the most common means of hanging and displaying curtains, but they are not always the most effective. Some windows will really benefit from the freshness and individuality of an innovative curtain heading. Fabric tabs looped on to a thick wooden pole can look as formal or informal as you please, depending on the curtain style and the choice of fabric. Alternatively, you can create a more dramatic effect by using

▼ **Make a point**
This luxurious striped curtain is attached to the pole with matching tabs, each of which has been tailored to a point and carefully positioned to emphasize the fabric design.

luxurious tassel-trimmed cord or ribbon, threaded through eyelets in the curtain, to secure it to the pole.

The curtain ideas featured here all give full coverage of the window when drawn, but use far less fabric than a tape heading, even when extra widths are added for fullness. Hang heavy curtains from thick wooden poles with ornately carved finials, or from slimmer iron poles for a more authentic rustic feel. Though most of the styles shown here can be pulled back along the pole, they look best when drawn either partially or fully across the window, then secured at the sides with matching tiebacks.

The fabric tabs can be made in the same fabric as the curtain, or in a contrasting colour and pattern; you can even use two or more fabrics for the heading tabs, either in toning or contrasting shades, depending on how striking an effect is wanted.

Measuring up

When using a fabric tab or eyelet heading, the curtain is usually hung just below the pole, rather than on it. Ensure you have at least a 5cm (2in) gap between the pole and the top of the window to accommodate the tabs, otherwise the tab headings will allow light to filter through at the top of the window.

To calculate the length of the actual curtain, measure from a point 5cm (2in) below the base of the pole, to just below the window or to the floor, as preferred. Add 3cm (1¼in) to the length for heading and hem allowances.

The curtain width depends on how full an effect is wanted when the curtains are drawn. For curtains that lie flat against the window, you will only need fabric the width of the window, plus extra for side seams and joining fabric widths. For a fuller effect, add a half or a whole fabric width to each curtain.

Materials

Fabric for curtains (for quantities see *Measuring up*)
Lining or **contrast fabric** if required
Matching sewing threads
Tape measure
Tailor's chalk

SIMPLE TAB HEADING

The instructions given here are for lined curtains.

1 **Making up the curtains** Measure the window area as described, and cut out the curtain fabric and lining to the correct size, joining fabric widths where necessary. With right sides together and edges matching, pin, tack and stitch the lining to the main fabric down both sides and across the lower edge, taking a 1.5cm (⅝in) seam allowance. Turn right side out.

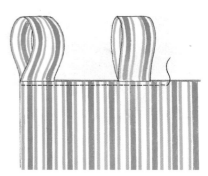

2 **Spacing the tabs** Decide how wide you would like the tabs to be – generally 5-7.5cm (2-3in). Then measure across the top of each curtain to see how many tabs you will need – you should begin and end with a tab, and allow approximately twice a tab's width for the spaces in-between. Use tailor's chalk to mark the position of each tab on the lining side of the curtain.

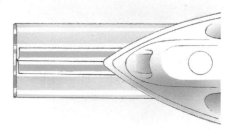

3 **Stitching the tabs** For each tab, cut one strip of your chosen fabric, 23cm (9in) long, and twice as wide as the finished tab plus 2cm (¾in). With right sides together, fold each tab in half lengthways and stitch down the long edges, taking a 1cm (⅜in) seam allowance. Centre the seam on the tab, open out the allowances and press. Turn the tabs right side out and press their edges into a sharp crease.

4 **Attaching the tabs** Lay out the curtain right side face up, and fold in 1.5cm (⅝in) of both the lining and the main fabric along the top edge. Fold each tab in half widthways, with the seam on the inside. Pin in place along the top of the curtain, slipping the raw ends of each tab in-between the lining and the main fabric, for 1.5cm (⅝in). Top stitch across top of curtain to attach both the lining and the tabs.

UNLINED CURTAINS

A tab heading can also be easily attached to unlined curtains, by means of a top facing.

1 **Preparing the facing** Hem the sides and bottom edge of the curtain, and make up the tabs as usual. Cut a facing 11cm (4¼in) deep and as wide as the curtain, plus 2cm (¾in), then cut and apply iron-on interfacing. Stitch a 1.5cm (⅝in) hem along the bottom edge of the facing.

2 **Attaching the tabs** Fold the tabs in half widthways and pin in place on the right side of the curtain, matching raw edges. Lie the facing over the tabs, wrong side up. Tack then stitch across the curtain top, through the facing, the tabs and the main fabric, taking a 1.5cm (⅝in) seam allowance. Flip the facing over to lie against the wrong side of the curtain, turn in 1cm (⅜in) of the facing at each side and slipstitch to the curtain's side hem to finish.

GATHERED TABS

A gathered tab heading will create a full curtain, which falls in soft folds when drawn across the pole. Make the tabs and their gathering bands in the same fabric as the main curtain, or use fabrics in toning or contrasting shades.

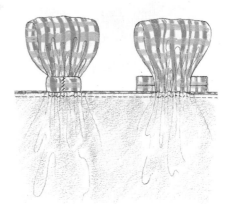

1 Marking up the tabs Make up the curtains as usual, leaving the top edges unstitched. In this design, each tab is double the usual width, so that it measures 11-15cm (4¼-6in); the space left in-between each tab is the same width as the finished tab. Mark the position of the tabs on the wrong side of each curtain.

2 Stitching the tabs For each tab, cut out a strip of your chosen fabric 23cm (9in) long and twice the width of the finished tab, plus 2cm (¾in). Stitch the tabs as before, and attach them to the curtain top.

◀ *Gathered for fullness*
Gathered tab headings are as simple to make as plain tabs, but create a far softer, fuller curtain.

3 Gathering the tabs For each tab, cut a fabric strip 11 x 6cm (4¼ x 2¼in). Fold each strip in half and stitch, as for tabs, with a 5mm (¼in) seam allowance. Turn through to right side and place one over the base of each tab, with seam underneath. Draw the ends of the strip round to the back of the tab, gathering up the tab as you go, and slipstitch strip ends together, folding in the raw ends. Hold in place at the bottom of the tab with a few stitches.

SPLIT-LEVEL TABS

Here the curtains are made up from two panels, one slightly larger than the other, and matching tabs provide a decorative link over the top. For the best results, choose toning fabrics and use the lighter of the two for the back panel.

1 Cutting out Measure the window as before. For each curtain, cut a piece of the light coloured back panel fabric to the desired finished size, plus 11.5cm (4½in) all round, and one of the front panel fabric to the finished size, plus 1.5cm (⅝in) all round; join widths where necessary.

2 Hemming the panels On the back panel, turn and press an 11.5cm (4½in) hem to wrong side all round the curtain; tack in place, mitring the corners and slipstitching them together for a neat finish. Repeat on front panel, taking a 6.5cm (2½in) hem.

3 Stitching the tabs Calculate how many tabs are needed, and mark their positions; the first and last tabs are placed slightly in from the sides of the front panel, and the spaces are twice as wide as the finished tabs. For each tab, cut a strip from your main fabric, 44.5cm (17½in) long and twice as wide as the tab, plus 2cm (¾in). Stitch tabs as before.

4 Making up the curtain With wrong sides together, centre front panel over back panel and tack then topstitch together down sides and along the lower edge, 10cm (4in) in from the curtain edge to make a flap, but enclosing raw edges.

5 Attaching the tabs Turn in 1.5cm (⅝in) at one end of each tab and slipstitch to close. Pin tabs in place across curtain top, with neatened ends against right side of back panel, and raw ends slipped in-between back and front panels. Both tab ends must lie 11.5cm (4½in) in from the top edge. Top stitch across curtain top, 10cm (4in) from top edge, securing tabs as you join panels. Remove tacking stitches.

▲ *Colourful combination*
Depending on the fabrics used to make this unusual tabbed curtain, various effects can be achieved. Back the front panel with a wide lacy border to create a soft feminine look, or use plain or striped fabrics for more modern settings.

Threaded eyelet headings

Striking headings can be created by inserting large eyelets into the top of the curtain, and threading these with lengths of cord or ribbon which are looped over the pole. Large eyelet kits can be bought from department stores and come complete with detailed fixing instructions. The eyelets are usually available in silver or bronze, so choose the colour that best complements your fabric.

Always insert the eyelets through a double layer of fabric and, unless your fabric is very thick, strengthen the top of the curtain with interfacing. These curtains cannot be drawn open, so use decorative tiebacks to fix them at the sides.

▲ Bound to impress
This heavy, textured kelim fabric is bound to its ornate gold-painted pole by a length of richly coloured cord. A pair of sumptuous wool tassels casually looped over the pole end hold it in place and complete the effect. To finish tie back the curtain with tassels.

▲ Two-tone heading
Use a length of pretty ribbon or braid to bind a fresh, summery curtain to its pole. As both sides of the ribbon will be visible, either use a ribbon that is double-sided, or stick two lengths together using a fabric bonder, as here. To add interest and colour and to strengthen the curtain top, line the curtain with a contrast fabric, which will be visible when the curtain sides are tied back.

◄ Metallic effect
Rather than binding your curtains to the pole with lengths of cord or ribbon, use split metal curtain rings, which can be slipped through the eyelets and looped on to the pole. As well as cleverly extending the metal eyelet theme, the rings will also enable you to draw the curtain back and forth across the pole.

Valance variations

A valance, trimmed with frills, binding, braid or fringing, gives an attractive finish to the window dressing, and works particularly well when balanced with tiebacks trimmed to match. The softly flowing shape of a valance helps to relax the hard lines of the window, adding volume and movement. It is a soft style and should not be confused with the smooth, stiff and tailored style of a pelmet.

In addition to their decorative value, valances have a double function in concealing the curtain track and helping to enhance the proportions of the window. The standard valance is one sixth of the length of the main curtains, and extends about 6cm (2½in) on each side. A valance which is longer than usual helps to balance a tall window, while a very full valance can add width to windows of any height.

▲ **Country co-ordination**
This lovely, frilled valance, combined with matching curtains and a co-ordinating Austrian blind, gives this room a real country feel. The valance makes the window look shorter, but wider, like traditional cottage windows, and covers the curtain track for a neat finish.

Fitting a valance

A valance is basically just a short curtain, but it spans the full width of the window and is never drawn back. Like a curtain, it can be made using any number of curtain tapes, from simple gathers to triple or cartridge pleats, and like a curtain it can be hung at the window in a number of ways.

The easiest way to hang a valance is on a valance track, which runs in front of the main track and extends slightly on each side, covering the main track completely. A number of curtain track manufacturers produce these, usually as optional fittings which use standard curtain hooks and can be added to certain curtain tracks when required.

When the main curtain track is fixed inside a window recess, instead of using a valance track, a slightly longer curtain track, pole or rod can be fixed just in front of the recess, and the valance attached to this. Another option for attaching valances is to use a pelmet shelf, but this will be covered in a later chapter.

MAKING A SIMPLE VALANCE

1 Planning the effect A standard proportion for a valance is one sixth of the length of the main curtain. Cut a piece of paper this size and position it at the window to check the effect. If you wish to make a tall window seem shorter, make the valance longer, but to let in maximum light, make the valance shorter. Decide also on the heading tape you prefer – it doesn't have to be the same as the tape used for the curtains.

2 Cutting out Cut out strips of fabric the width of the fabric by the length of the finished valance plus 20cm (8in). The number of widths you need depends on the heading tape; cut out enough widths to make up a piece the required size, making sure the pattern will match across seams. Remember, the valance goes round both sides, so include these in your measurements.

Join the fabric widths together, taking 1.5cm (⅝in) seam allowances and stitching the fabric with right sides together: press seams open.

3 Adding a lining For a lined valance, cut out and join the lining fabric to make a piece 8cm (3in) shorter and 4cm (1½in) narrower than the main fabric. Lightly press the seams open.

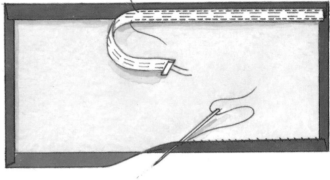

4 Stitching the valance Make up the valance in the same way as a curtain using a plain or decorative curtain tape. For a simple, unlined valance, follow the instructions on page 93. For a lined valance, follow the instructions for a curtain with sewn-in lining on page 94.

5 Hanging the valance Pull up the cords in the heading tape to fit the valance track and knot. Insert the appropriate curtain hooks into the tape and slip through the rings on the valance track to hang. If using a curtain pole or rod at a recessed window, attach the valance to this in the same way.

▶ *Valance elegance*
Even a simple valance with narrow heading can look smart. This lovely version, edged at top and bottom with pretty pink bias binding, adds width to this elegant landing window, and gives it a simple, but classic look.

Depth gauge
Let the depth of the pattern repeat on the fabric dictate the exact depth of the valance – if one or more pattern repeats fit the depth, it gives the valance a professional finish.

A LINE AND FRILLED VALANCE

1 Cutting the fabric Cut out widths of fabric the finished length of the valance, with pattern repeats matching. Since the frill will add to the length, there is no need to add seam allowances at top and bottom. The width of the fabric depends on the heading tape – twice the finished width is average. Cut and join enough widths to make up a piece the required size, taking 1.5cm (⅝in) seam allowances. Cut and join the lining fabric to make a piece the same size.

2 Cutting the frill For a frill 6cm (2½in) deep, cut widths of fabric, with pattern repeats matching, 15cm (6in) deep to make up a piece two to two and a half times the measurement across the ungathered valance. Join the pieces together to make up one long strip, taking 1.5cm (⅝in) seam allowances and stitching with right sides together.

3 Making the frill Fold the strip of fabric in half lengthways, right sides together, and stitch across the ends, taking a 1.5cm (⅝in) seam allowance. Trim the seams and turn right side out, re-folding the fabric in half lengthways; press.

▲ Short and sweet
A very attractive way of finishing a valance on a border fabric is to stitch round the design on the lower edge with narrow, close zigzag and then trim close to the stitching. This pretty effect looks particularly attractive when the fabric is only lightly gathered.

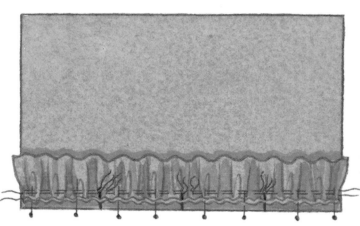

4 Attaching the frill Divide both the frill and lower edge of the valance into four and mark at the edges with tailor's chalk. Run two rows of gathering threads close to the raw edges of the frill, stopping and starting at marks. Pull up the threads to gather the frill to fit the valance, matching marks, but leaving 1.5cm (⅝in) free at each end for side seams. Pin and then tack 1cm (⅜in) from the raw edge.

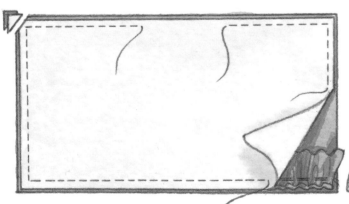

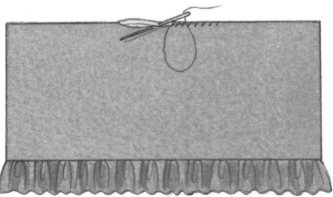

5 Attaching the lining Place the lining right side down on top of the valance and frill. Tack and then stitch together all round with raw edges level, taking a 1.5cm (⅝in) seam allowance and leaving a 20cm (8in) opening free on the top edge. Trim the seam allowances at the corners and then remove the tacking threads.

6 Finishing off Turn the valance right side out through the opening at the top edge and press. Oversew the opening closed with small stitches, then attach the heading tape to the lining side in the usual way (see page 93). Gather up and hang the valance on the track.

DECORATIVE OPTIONS

A curtain valance offers an excellent opportunity for using one of the many attractive trimmings on the market. Here are just a few to give you inspiration.

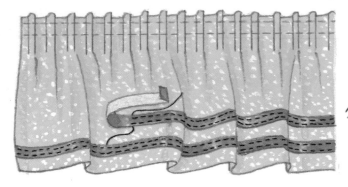

Ribbon trim Make a simple valance, and then purchase enough ribbon to go along the full width of the valance plus 3cm (1¼in). Turn the ends under, pin in position on the valance and then stitch in place along both long edges. Add a second row of ribbon if you like.

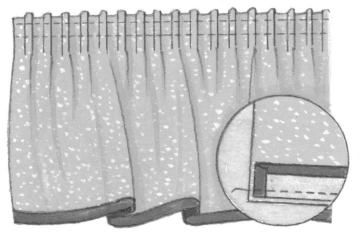

Bound edge Cut out and join the fabric to make up a valance the required width (depending on the tape used) by the finish length plus 4cm (1½in). Turn double 1cm (⅜in) hems to the wrong side along each side edge, then turn down 4cm (1½in) at the top and attach the heading tape. Attach bias binding to the lower edge (see page 46).

For a lined and bound valance, cut out the fabric and lining as for a frilled valance. Place the main fabric and lining right sides together, then stitch along both sides and the top edge, taking a 1.5cm (⅝in) seam. Turn right side out, pin the two fabrics together and then finish the lower edge with the binding.

Contrast trim Decide on the finished width of the trim, then make up a valance as for a bound edge, adding a 1.5cm (⅝in) seam allowance but deducting the depth of the trim from the length. Cut out and join fabric widths from the trimming fabric, twice the required finished depth plus 3cm (1¼in), matching the pattern repeats. Join to make up a piece the same width as the valance fabric. Fold both long edges 1.5cm (⅝in) to the wrong side, and attach like binding. Stitch the ends of the trim together with slipstitches, with seam allowances inside.

For a lined, trimmed valance, make up like a lined, bound valance, adding a 1.5cm (⅝in) seam allowance and deducting the depth of the trim from the cut length. Attach the trimming like binding.

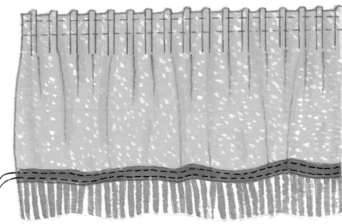

Fringing Cut out and make a simple valance. For a lined valance, follow the instructions for the frilled valance, but omit the frill. Cut a length of fringing long enough to go across the width of the ungathered valance plus 2cm (¾in). Turn each end under, pin to the valance and then stitch the fringing to the valance along each long edge.

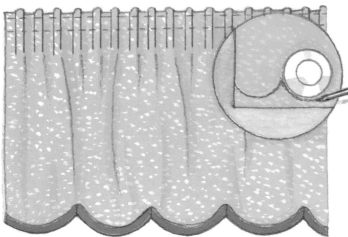

Scalloped edge Cut out and join the fabric as for a bound edge, then using a plate as a template, draw scallops on the wrong side at the lower edge of the main fabric; cut out. Turn double 1cm (⅜in) hems to the wrong side along each side edge, then turn 4cm (1½in) at the top and attach the heading tape. Attach binding to the lower edge, easing round curves and folding binding at the top of the scallops.

For a lined, scalloped valance, cut out and make up as for a lined, bound valance, then cut the lower edge of fabric and lining into scallops before binding.

118

Formal fabric pelmets

Pelmets give windows an elegant, tailored look which is ideal for dining rooms and other formal areas of the home. Like valances, they are placed at the top of the window, defining the curtain arrangement and covering the curtain track, even when the curtains are drawn back. Unlike valances, which are soft and flowing, pelmets are made from wood or fabric stiffened with buckram or self-adhesive stiffener.

Wooden pelmets are usually fairly straight across the lower edge because it is difficult to cut complex patterns in the wood with accuracy, but with a fabric pelmet, you can make the shape as intricate as you like. Cut the edge into scallops, curves or waves for a soft, flowing effect, or shape it into turrets, like a castle, or ledges for a more formal effect. You can even cut round the shape of the design on the fabric for an unusual and really individual, tailor-made look.

Choosing a fabric

Most furnishing fabrics which are suitable for curtain-making can also be used for the pelmet. Cotton, chintz, ging-ham, brocade and even silk are suitable, but lightweight and loosely woven fabrics including sheers, lace and net are not – if you wish to use these, then choose a valance style instead.

▼ Making waves
The large, soft waves on this pelmet have been carefully cut out to complement the floral design of the fabric. Co-ordinated braid at the top and bottom of the pelmet give the whole thing a neat finish.

Choosing a stiffener

Buckram is traditionally used to stiffen the pelmet, and is combined with an additional layer of interlining to provide extra body and to make the finished pelmet look more luxurious. It has to be hand stitched in place, but the extra effort does mean that the finished pelmet will last well and can be washed or dry-cleaned as required.

Self-adhesive stiffener is the modern equivalent of buckram. It is made from strong, flexible pvc with a printed backing which contains several suggested designs already drawn to scale and full written instructions. It does not require interlining and is self-adhesive for quick results.

There are two types of self-adhesive stiffener to choose from – with an adhesive backing on one or both sides. Choose the type with one adhesive side for quick and economical results, or the type with adhesive on both sides if you wish to line the pelmet. Neither type can be washed or dry-cleaned, although some marks can be sponged off.

Using self-adhesive stiffener

Self-adhesive stiffener is easy to use, particularly if you wish to cut round one of the five pre-printed pelmet designs on the back. Even if you wish to make your own design, self-adhesive stiffener makes it easy by providing a grid to aid measurement and design. Choose one of three widths: 30cm (12in) for small windows, 40cm (16in) for standard windows, and 60cm (24in) for large windows, such as french windows.

▼ *Pre-printed design shapes*

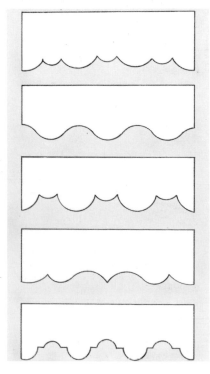

PRE-PRINTED DESIGNS

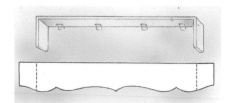

1 Measuring up Fix a pelmet box at the window. Measure the length of the pelmet front and sides for the total length of the pelmet. With the design on the self-adhesive stiffener centred, mark the required length. Mark where the pelmet turns the corner and check that the design looks good from the front. You may need to adjust the pattern at the sides for a neat effect. Cut to length, then cut along the lower edge, following the lines for your pattern.

2 Cutting the fabric Press the fabric to remove any wrinkles, then place the self-adhesive stiffener on the wrong side of the fabric with the pattern centred in the middle. Draw round the self-adhesive stiffener with tailor's chalk, then draw another line round this 2.5cm (1in) beyond. Check that the pattern works well with the shape of the self-adhesive stiffener, then cut out, following the outer chalk line.

On very wide windows it may be necessary to join fabric pieces together to make up the required width. If so, use a full fabric width in the middle with two smaller pieces at the sides. Join the fabric with right sides together and trim the allowances to 1cm (⅜in). Press seams open before cutting to shape.

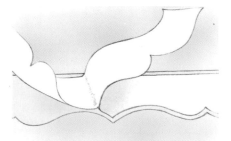

3 Sticking on the backing Starting at the *centre* of the self-adhesive stiffener, lift and then cut through the centre of the backing. Peel back part of the backing, then place on the wrong side of the fabric with the adhesive backing face down. Smooth the exposed adhesive on to the fabric, making sure there are no wrinkles in the fabric. Peel away the rest of the backing a little at a time, smoothing the backing on to the fabric as you do so.

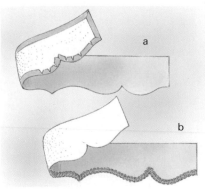

Single adhesive side Snip into the allowance all round 3mm (⅛in) from the self-adhesive stiffener and then turn the edges over to the wrong side. Carefully glue in place with fabric glue and leave to dry (a). Alternatively, trim the excess fabric close to the edge of the self-adhesive stiffener and stitch or glue braid along the bottom edge to finish (b). Attach the fixings to hang to the pelmet box above the window.

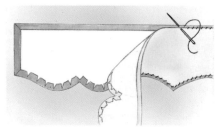

Both sides adhesive Snip into the fabric allowance all round 3mm (⅛in) from the self-adhesive stiffener. Peel the backing off the reverse of the self-adhesive stiffener and fold the excess fabric over, pressing on to the adhesive. Cut the lining the same size as the shaped self-adhesive stiffener. Press 1cm (⅜in) to the wrong side of the lining all round, then place wrong side down on top of the adhesive. Press in place carefully to avoid wrinkles. Slipstitch the lining to the fabric all round and attach the fixings to hang to the pelmet box.

Easy-hang pelmet

The type of self-adhesive stiffener which has one adhesive side only, has a soft backing on the non-adhesive side which will stick to the hook side of velcro. Simply glue the hook side of the velcro along the top edge of the pelmet box and press the pelmet in place.

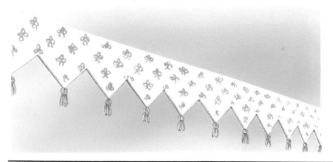
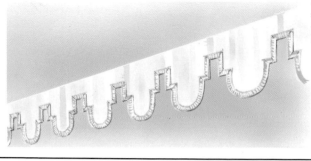

MAKING UP A DESIGN

1 Preparation. Fix a pelmet box at the window. Measure the length of the box and the depth of both sides. Add together, and cut a piece of self-adhesive stiffener this length. Mark the self-adhesive stiffener with the depth of the side at each end and mark the centre to ensure you obtain a symmetrical pattern.

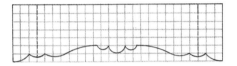

2 Making the design Draw your pattern on to the back of the self-adhesive stiffener so that it is centred across the pelmet front. Use the grid pattern on the self-adhesive stiffener to draw straight lines, and a french curve and circular object such as a cup to draw curves and scallops. When you are satisfied with the design, cut the self-adhesive stiffener to shape. Press the fabric, cut out and then make the pelmet, following the instructions for a pre-printed design.

USING THE PATTERN ON THE FABRIC

Border fabrics make attractive pelmets when the fabric is turned sideways to run across the top of the window. Use the width of the pattern repeat as a guide for the depth of the pelmet, using exactly one or more pattern repeats.

1 Applying the stiffener Fix a pelmet box at the window. Measure up and cut out the self-adhesive stiffener to the required length; do not trim the width. Cut out a strip of fabric 2.5cm (1in) larger than the self-adhesive stiffener all round, with the pattern centred widthways and with its lower edge 5cm (2in) above the lower edge of the fabric. Place the self-adhesive stiffener, backing side down, centred in the wrong side of the fabric. Peel away the backing from the centre of the self-adhesive stiffener and stick

to the fabric. Slowly peel back more of the backing until all the self-adhesive stiffener is firmly stuck to the fabric.

2 Making the pelmet Trim the excess fabric on the side edges flush with the self-adhesive stiffener. At the top edge, trim the fabric in a straight line just above the pattern, allowing sufficient depth beneath for the pelmet. Trim the lower edge in the same way and add a braid trim along each edge, if required.

▲ **Inspired by design**
This cleverly designed pelmet uses the pattern as a guide for its shape.

Shaped lower edge If preferred, neaten the top and side edges as in step 2 above, and then shape the lower edge round the pattern. To do this, carefully cut close to the pattern with sharp scissors or a craft knife. If the pattern is not too intricate, and you wish to trim it with a suitable braid, cut round the pattern the width of the trimming away from it. Glue or stitch the trimming in place (see page 118).

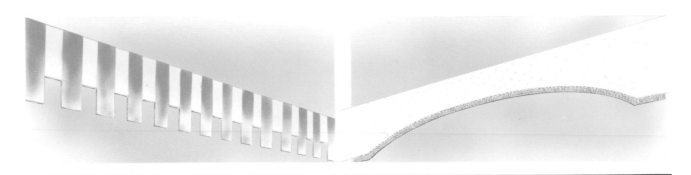

Buckram for pelmets

Buckram requires more hand stitching than self-adhesive stiffener, and you will have to make your own pattern before you start, but the end result has a softer look than one made with self-adhesive stiffener, and it should last longer because it can be cleaned. The pelmet should be about an eighth to a sixth of the length of the window, but standard depths are 30-40cm (12-16in) at the deepest points. It must also hide the track even at the highest points.

For your pattern, choose one of the designs given on the previous pages, or use the pattern of the fabric to provide inspiration for the shape.

USING BUCKRAM

1 Cutting out Cut a piece of dressmaker's squared paper or graph paper the required depth by the length of the pelmet box plus the sides. Mark the position of the side edges and centre. Design your pattern, then hold it up to the window to check the effect. Cut from buckram using the template as a guide. Cut again from fabric, adding 2.5cm (1in) all round; from interlining, adding 1.3cm (½in) all round; and from lining adding 1cm (⅜in) all round.

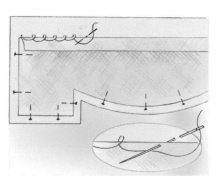

2 Attaching the interlining Centre the interlining on the wrong side of the main fabric and pin in the middle to hold. Lock stitch to the fabric by taking a small backstitch to pick up one thread from both the main fabric and interlining. Position the stitches 10cm (4in) apart and rows 30cm (12in) apart. This ensures the interlining will stay in place.

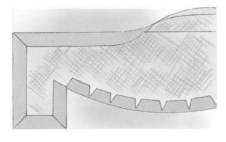

3 Attaching the buckram One side of the buckram is impregnated with glue. Dampen this side round the edges and then place on the interlining, this side up. Press the fabric allowances over the top all round, snipping into the allowances at corners and curves for ease.

4 Adding a trimming Stitch a trimming of braid or fringing to the pelmet before adding the lining to the back.

▲ **Trimming expertise**
A gathered trimming, is made into rosettes to emphasise the pelmet shape.

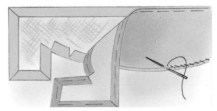

5 Attaching the lining Turn a 1.5cm (⅝in) seam allowance all round the lining so that it is slightly smaller than the main piece; tack. Pin centrally over the buckram and slipstitch together all round. Remove all the tacking stitches and attach the fixing to the back – the soft part of velcro, for example.

Swags and tails

Swags and tails are traditionally the reserve of grand houses and stately country homes, whose majestic windows demand lavish treatment. But although the style was devised with tall, slim windows in mind, it can very easily be adapted to suit all kinds of window shapes and sizes, whether tall or short, wide or narrow.

In a formal dining or living room where the windows are relatively large, swags and tails make an impressive crown for full-length curtains. To add definition and interest to an ornate arrangement, trim the swags and tails with a luxurious fringe, a full frill or decorative braid. For smaller windows and a less imposing effect, use swags and tails on their own to create a frame for the window and the view beyond it; if the window is overlooked, team them with a roller blind or sheer curtain.

Swags and tails are arranged to give the impression of a single length of fabric, draped across the window, but they are actually made up from three or more shaped pieces of fabric, assembled on a pelmet shelf above the window. The swag is cut on the bias so it forms natural, full folds when hung, and it can vary in depth depending on the window height and the desired effect. The tails which fall on each side of the swag can be spirals, flutes, asymmetrical (folding in from both tail sides) or the more common triangular cut, with staggered folds down one side only. To emphasize the folds and to give the tails a full, rounded appearance, they are usually lined with a contrasting fabric.

▼ **Bedroom flair**
In this stylish bedroom, swags and tails crown luxurious full-length curtains, to add emphasis and authority to the window. The arrangement adds a touch of grandeur, without being overly formal.

Proportioning the arrangement

There are no fixed rules for proportioning a swag and tail arrangement in relation to the window, but the following guidelines are worth bearing in mind. To avoid a top-heavy appearance, the swag should be no longer than about one-sixth of the window drop, particularly where the window is small and allows little light into the room.

The tails should fall halfway to two-thirds down the window, or even further where the arrangement is being used without curtains. The first pleat of each tail should lie at roughly the same level as the lowest point of the swag. Before you begin, take a look at several pictures to get an idea of the different effects that can be created for your shape and style of window.

Materials

Fabric for the swags and tails. (See instructions for quantities.)
Contrast lining to back swags and tails
Length of plywood 9mm (⅜in) thick, 10cm (4in) wide and slightly longer than your window, to make a pelmet shelf; the swags and tails are assembled on the shelf and attached to it
38mm (1½in) steel angle brackets, 1cm (⅜in) and 3.2cm (1¼in) woodscrews with wallplugs for fixing the brackets to the pelmet shelf and wall
Sew 'n' Stick Velcro one and a half times the length of the pelmet shelf
Tape measure
Matching sewing threads

▲ *Elegantly framed* Swags and tails need not always be teamed with curtains, but look just as stunning used alone or with a simple roller blind. This type of arrangement is ideal for the striking bathroom shown here, which calls for a lavish treatment, but where space around the window is too limited for curtains.

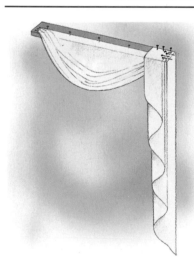

5 Shaping the tails Hang the tail in place over the pelmet shelf, covering one pleated end of the swag. Arrange the folds and pin them in place, adjusting the fabric and trimming it where necessary, until you are satisfied with the finished effect. Step back and check that the swag and tail arrangement works well as a whole, before taking down both pattern pieces.

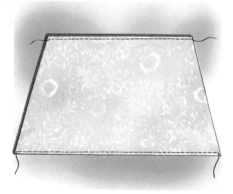

6 Making up the swag The swag is often cut on the bias to create softer, more natural folds. Using your fabric pattern as a guide and adding a 1.5cm (⅝in) seam allowance all round, cut out the swag from your main fabric and lining. With right sides together and edges matching, pin and stitch the lining to the main fabric along the top and bottom edges, taking a 1.5cm (⅝in) seam allowance. Trim the seam allowances, turn the swag through to the right side and press.

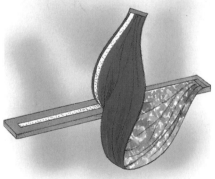

7 Fixing the swag Gather or pleat up the ends of the swag on the pelmet shelf as you did before with the fabric pattern. Once satisfied with the effect, hold the folds in place with a few stitches at the sides; take down the swag and machine stitch the folds in place at the sides, trim and bind the raw edges for a neat finish. Stitch the stitching half of the Velcro along the top of the swag, and stick the other half to the top of the pelmet shelf. Fix the swag in place on the shelf.

SWAGS AND TAILS

The instructions given below are for a single swag and two triangular tails with three staggered pleats. Both the swag and the tails are lined with a contrast fabric to create a fuller effect and to emphasize the pleats on the tails.

1 Fixing the pelmet shelf Use the angle brackets to attach the pelmet shelf above the window, ready to carry the swag and tails. An arrangement of swags and tails on a small window can block out light, so fix the shelf well above it and make sure it extends beyond the window on both sides, this also makes the window look larger.

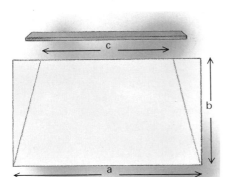

2 Measuring up for the swag First decide how far down the window you want the swag to hang. Using an

old sheet to make a pattern, cut a rectangle from it 20cm (8in) longer than the shelf **(a)**, by 1½ times the depth of the finished swag, plus 5cm (2in) for attaching it to the top of the shelf **(b)**. Measure 20cm (8in) in from each side along one long edge, and mark. Join these points to the two corners on the other long edge and trim along the lines; the top edge of the pattern **(c)** will then be 20cm (8in) shorter than the shelf.

3 Shaping the swag Fix the swag pattern piece in place on the pelmet shelf, attaching it to the top of the shelf with a few temporary tacks; knock the tacks in halfway only, for easy removal. Pleat up the side ends of the swag pattern piece to form soft sweeping folds across the window; pin the folds in place slightly in from the ends of the shelf, where they will be covered by the tails. Adjust the arrangement until you are happy with it, and trim the fabric where necessary.

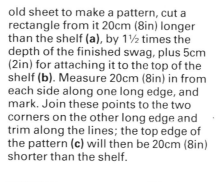

4 Measuring up for the tails Decide how long and wide the tails will be, and how many pleats they will have. Following our pattern for three 18cm (7in) pleats, cut a fabric pattern piece as follows: width across top **(d)** = 18cm (7in) x 7 (number of folds) + 10cm (4in) to wrap around the shelf ends; length of outer edge **(e)** = depth of tail + 7.5cm (3in) for fixing to shelf; length of inner edge **(f)** = depth of finished swag + 7.5cm (3in) for fixing to shelf. The tail's lower edge is cut diagonally to create the staggered pleats. Mark up the foldlines as shown.

---

8 Cutting out the tails For each tail, use the pattern to cut out one piece of main fabric and one of lining, adding a 1.5cm (⅝in) seam allowance all round. Flip the pattern piece over to cut out the second tail, to give two mirror images.

9 Making up the tails With right sides together and edges matching, stitch the lining fabric to the main fabric for each tail, down both sides and along the slanted lower edge, taking a 1.5cm (⅝in) seam allowance. Trim the seam allowances, clip the corners, turn through to the right side and press.

Alternative fixing

To save time, use staples and a staple gun rather than Velcro to fix the swags and tails in place on the pelmet shelf.

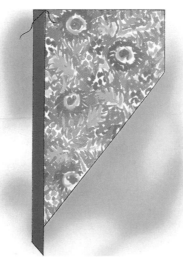

10 A neat fit Lay out one tail with right side face up, and fold in that part of the outer side edge which will extend around the side of the pelmet shelf. Make a dart by stitching through all layers of fabric, from the outer corner of the shelf to the top corner of the tail. The tail will then fit neatly around the corner. Repeat on the other tail.

11 Fixing the tails Pleat up the tails on the pelmet shelf as before, checking the effect. Once satisfied, hold the pleats in place with a few stitches. Take down the tails and machine stitch folds in place along edge; trim top edge if necessary and bind or oversew raw edges. Attach Velcro to underside of the tails, and to the shelf, as for the swags, and fix tails in place.

Informal arrangements

In settings where swags and tails would be too formal, opt for an equally impressive but more casual approach, in which the window is framed by a single length of fabric draped to suit its style and shape. The finished effect can be as simple or elaborate as you please, from a single short fabric length used to crown a small picture window, to great swathes of fabric, draped around French windows and left to fall in abundant folds to the ground.

Like swags and tails, these types of arrangement can be used with or without curtains or a blind. On large windows, the fabric is generally draped over a decorative wooden pole, and fixed in place with tacks where necessary. Here, the pole should be extended beyond the window on each side, to avoid cutting out too much light, and to create the illusion of a larger window. Contrast line the fabric to give it volume and to emphasize its folds as it is twisted and draped around the pole.

On smaller windows which carry less lavish arrangements, the fabric can either be attached to a pelmet shelf as previously described, or alternative fixing techniques can be used, such as metal or plastic coils attached either side of the window.

▲ **Swathed in fabric**
This asymmetrical arrangement, teamed with matching full-length curtains, adds a touch of luxury to the modest surroundings. The fabric is lined, and the ends have been shaped to form the staggered pleats of a classic tail. The contrast lining also provides a decorative border for the main fabric.

◄ **Crowning glory**
This charming variation on a swag and tail arrangement is formed from a single long strip of unlined fabric. The fabric is simply pulled through metal or plastic coils fixed either side of the window, and then scrunched up to form full rosettes. The ends are left to hang in two short tails.

Index

Page numbers in *italic* refer to picture captions

Acknowledgements

Photographers: Ametex UK Ltd 85, 99; Bo Appeltofft 62, 126(b); Ariadne Holland 25; Laura Ashley 87; Brooke London Ltd 11; Co-op 102; Crown Paints 107; Crownson Fabrics FC 103, 126(t); Jane Churchill Ltd 70(t); Cy De Cosse 22, 46, 104, 106; Dorma Fabrics Ltd 15-16, 47, 63; Dulux Paints Ltd 39, 45; Eaglemoss Publications Ltd (Sue Atkinson) 31-34, (Marie-Louise Avery) 74(b), 117, (Eric Crichton) 17, (Simon Butcher) 80, 124, (Tiff Hunter) 88-89, (Simon Page-Ritchie) 23-24, 26, 48-50, 108, (John Suett) 35-36, 38 (Steve Tanner) 7-8, 10, 12-13, 18, 58, 72-74, 76-77, 83-84, 114(t&c); Forbo Mayfair Ltd 98(br); Anna French Ltd 55, 73(bl), 113(b); Robert Harding Picture Library 29, 105; Harrison Drape Ltd 115-116; Hill & Knowles Ltd 111, 113(t); Interior Selection 14, 121; Kirsch 71; Maison de Marie Claire 66(t&b), 114(b); Marks & Spencer Plc 91, 98(c); Monkwell Fabrics Ltd 30; Osborne & Little Plc 56-57, 67, 70(br), 122; Richard Paul 21, 27-28, 59-61(1), 92, 97(r); Pictures Colour Library 51; Romo Fabrics 19, 119; Sanderson & Sons Ltd 40, 42-43; B & R Stoeltie 61(r), 70(bl); Tino Tedaldi 68; Warner Fabrics 123; EWA (Michael Crockett) 82 (b), (Michael Dunne) 66(c); (Tom Leighton) 54, (Di Lewis) 65, 90, 95, (Neil Lorimer) 79, (Spike Powell) 96-97(1), 98(bl), (Jerry Tubby) 82(t); Ashley Wilde Designs 110.

Illustrators: Julie-Ann Burt 24(t), 25(br); Christine Hart-Davies 41-42, 60-62; Terry Evans 12-14, 24(b), 25 (bl), 26, 36-38, 52-54, 78(b), 84-86, 108-110, 116-118; Will Giles & Sarah Pond 20-22, 44-46, 93-94, 96-97, 100-102, 104-106; John Hutchinson 8-10, 32-34, 47-50, 56-58, 64-65, 68-69, 112-113, 120-122, 124-125; Irwin Technical 76-78(t); Stan North 89-90; Kate Simunek 16-18, 28-30.